A collection of works by
and Badenoch Herald's least favourite scribe.

Foolscap
brought to book

[or - 'The Rude, The Mad and The Smugly']

Since April 1993, Foolscap has terrorised the citizenry of the Badenoch and Strathspey area with his incisive wit and acerbic tongue.

Now at last it is possible to read the collection of some of the best (and worst) of his work from over the years.

Solas Publications

6 Bank Street, Plockton
Wester Ross, Scotland

First published in Great Britain in 1999 by Solas Publications

a division of

Solas Business Services Ltd

6 Bank Street Plockton, Ross-shire IV52 8TP

ISBN 0 9537362 0 2

Cover Design by Karen Gordon

Leroi Design

27 Dalmaik Terrace, Peterculter, Aberdeen AB14 0TQ

Printed and bound in Great Britain by

Highland Printers Ltd

13 Henderson Road, Longman North,Inverness IV1 1SP

Foolscap
brought to book

[or - 'The Rude, The Mad and The Smugly']

CONTENTS

Preview Reviews vi
Acknowledgements vii
Publisher's Note viii
Introduction 1
In the Beginning 3
1993 .5
1994 22
1995 49
1996 65
1997 90
1998 108
1999 128
Author's Note 146

PREVIEW REVIEWS

Foolscap brought to book *is anticipating a chorus of enthusiastic reviews. A few examples:-*

"An invaluable insight into the culture of rural Highland life"
Piotr Steinlovitch in *KGB Today*

"Many interesting variants in the use of the English Language"
Patagonian Educational Supplement

"A highly recommended read - and excellent value for money too"
F.S. in *Strathspey and Badenoch Herald*

"Anonymity is the strongest weapon in the whinger's armoury. Thank you, Foolscap. You are an example to us all"
Mole Yearbook, 1999

"We are monitoring sales of this book with interest"
Paper Pulpers & Recyclers Gazette

"An amazing anecdotal anthology"
Aviemore Alliterative Association Almanac

ACKNOWLEDGEMENTS

Previously published cartoons by Foolscap

Original cartoons for this publication by Lorna Bruce

Pageset in Adobe Pagemaker 6.52®
by AXXESS (Highland) Limited, Newtonmore

Thanks also to Scott Bruce for arranging publication
and checking the copy for spelling and tyqografical errors.

We make no apologies for any omissions but wish to thank
many of those who are not mentioned for their kind donations
to the Foolscap Benevolent Fund.

PUBLISHER'S NOTE

In time-honoured fashion, we wish to point out that the characters in this book are fictitious and any resemblance in name or action to real or living people is, of course, entirely coincidental.

INTRODUCTION

Journalism is, they say, the first draft of history. And when the story of 20th Century Badenoch and Strathspey comes to be written in future, it will be to this collection of the writings of Foolscap that historians will turn first. They will then immediately turn away, realising they actually meant to look Over There, but no matter.

Today the idle reader (and Olympic Standard Idleness would need to have been achieved before finally alighting on this work) will find inside a unique portrait of the exotic lives of the power brokers, fat cats, lissom beauties and style icons who populate the Fast Lane in Strathspey and Badenoch. And there are bits about some 'cooncillors' too.

Even though I am personally known to the publisher (but still found myself vilified and referred to in unflattering terms in the famous Strathie columns), I can heartily recommend this publication. One can never have too many doorstops.

BBC Radio 2
Broadcasting House
Regent Street
London

IN THE
BEGINNING ....

*F*oolscap first saw the light of day in April 1993. At the end *of the first year, in December 1993, I wrote the following piece, which has since proved to be spookily prophetic.*

I suggest to Editor Ken Smith that, in common with other newspaper diarists, I get into the Christmas book market by publishing 'The Best of Foolscap' but he points out that there may not be a big market for a two page pamphlet. He goes on to say that we could just about run to this size providing we have a plain white cover and a drawing of me on one of the inside pages. Undaunted, I ask him if he thinks I should put more fire into my work. "No," he replied with unnecessary candour, "Quite the reverse."

Over the years a number of friends, moles and enemies have suggested that I should produce just such a volume but until now I have never felt that Highland literary taste had declined so far as to make it a feasible venture. I can only say that I have changed my mind because the prospect of untold wealth has been dangled before me by an unscrupulous publisher anxious only to make his own name in breaking new ground and attempting to attract a jaded public palate with the following load of drivel. Just what sort of people would buy such a book has never been entirely clear and I will anxiously scour the news-stands to identify the type of people loose in our society who will spend good money on works of such dubious literary worth.

However, who am I to judge the taste of others. If you absolutely insist on going ahead and reading this, I can only say, Good Luck. Oh yes. And thanks for buying the book. That untold wealth may yet be within my grasp.

The best place to start is at the beginning and so our first few pieces are from the very first Foolscap back in 1993 on the 29th of April

1993

Beadh an Braighfasghd. What a wonderful language is the Gaelic and how nice it is to listen to the Grampian Television News spoken in this evocative tongue every day. Just a pity that only about 2% of the area's viewing public can understand a single word of it. I realise now that had I stuck in at the Gaelic instead of chasing girls in my youth, I wouldn't be in half the trouble I am now. For a variety of different reasons! Budget! That's the important word. With a budget for Gaelic Broadcasting running into millions I would have been able to get my hands on some of it instead of working in this minority language, English. Gaelic Broadcasting is certainly a burgeoning market for anyone with a little knowledge of the tongue not to mention the equally important knowledge of where to stick it.

****

From time to time correspondence arrives at Foolscap's 10th floor penthouse suite at Strathie Towers our beautiful new HQ building in Grantown. Dropping on to the leather topped Sheraton desk today comes this note from a distant reader.

Dear Sir,

As a direct descendant of Johann Lunz the famous cartographer who did so much to open up the Scottish Highlands with his Atlas Novus of 1659 perhaps I can help in the acrimonious correspondence regarding the correct spelling of Carrbridge, or indeed Carr-Bridge.

Curiously enough Lunz originally had the place named Manchester but unfortunately there was some confusion with another place of the same name somewhere in England which as far as I know is still there. After the 'Coffin Bridge was built in 1717 the residents on the north side named the area Ghurrbhreadhgth which I understand is Gaelic for 'lousy bridge where stinking south bank peasants hang about and spit at travellers especially on early closing day.' This last version, I think, must take precedence as the correct spelling. I trust that this helps to clear up the problem for your readers.

Yours etc.

The Hon. Percy Wilberforce Cattermole-Lunz.

Dunmappin

Havering-in-the-Field.

Hants.

****

6

As 'Echoes from the Past' is a favourite 'Herald' feature, this column thought it only right in the interests of fairness that the future should occasionally get its say.

ECHOES FROM THE FUTURE
It will happen in 25 years and will appear in the Strathspey and Badenoch Herald on Friday April 25th 2018.

The 57th planning application for a supermarket in Aviemore is announced. The committee who have been pondering this problem now for nearly thirty years say that this time they are sure they will be able to make a decision despite the fact that many of their number have succumbed to the grim reaper over the last 15 years.

Conservation Police announced today that a Nethybridge man was shot by guards as he attempted to climb over the Cairngorm Ring Fence. The man who has not been named is recovering in Raigmore Hospital but faces life imprisonment for this heinous crime. He is reported to have said "I just wanted to see the mountains once more before I die." His wife and family are moving out of the area to start a new life under a different name. After the first cold Winter in many years plans are released today by the Tourist Board suggesting that local businesses could benefit from the sport of ski-ing and that the area could become an all year round resort. The Chairman of the Aviemore Community Council Mr. Ian Malcolm (70), who can remember working for the old Cairngorm Chairlift company said that as far as he knew the machinery was still there and that National Heritage had kept

7

it perfectly preserved as a museum although as it was within the prohibited area it may not be possible to use it. Tourist Board Committee member Mr. Sandy Caird (89) said, "It's a damn good idea and local people should bloody well get behind it." He immediately had a seizure and was carried out to the Old Bridge Inn to recover.

****

And from here, it is a motley collection following the order in which the pieces were first published

Grantown has a certain charm which attracts that portion of the population which has done its bit and now wants to sit down with its feet up. So many people have retired here over the years that it has become something of an elephant's graveyard where the genteel middle classes from the south, come to die. Most recently it has taken great favour with retiring military types and is now so full of Lt. Colonels, Squadron Leaders and others of that ilk that one unkind humorist of this column's acquaintance claims that on most days the High Street can be brought to a complete standstill just by shouting Atten......SHUN.

****

8

Fans of Shakespeare Dept. Because this column has an erudite following it goes to the ends of the earth to find interesting literary anecdotes. This week we travel to the U.S.A. for the benefit of our readers where we found the following misquote from the bard on a sign in a Mid West Sporting goods store:

'Now is the discount of our winter tents!'

****

The Foolscap staff were glued to their TV sets avidly watching Grampian Television's Quiz show 'TOP CLUB' on the 14th of May. For those of you who missed the match between Spey Valley Rotary and Texaco Allstars here is a report from Foolscap's own 'Man on the Couchline'.

Local polymaths Ken Smith (Our handsome loveable editor) [how about that pay rise?] [No.Ed.] Bill Quirie and Alan Keegan fought bravely against insuperable odds (A smarter team) and managed after a closely run game to snatch defeat from the jaws of victory in a tension packed thirty minutes. The fans (Mrs Smith, Mrs Quirie & Mrs.Keegan) went wild at the end of the match, storming onto the studio floor drinking cups of tea. There were a few scuffles but no arrests. We wuz definitely robbed and the boys were sick as parrots. We can only assume that the lads from Texaco were over the moon.

Score: Texaco Allstars - 1, Spey Valley Rotary - Lost.

ECHOES FROM THE FUTURE

A further step in the programme of introducing useful and benign additives to the nation's water supply, which started with fluoridation in the last century was announced today. Because of the upsurge in Scottish Nationalism in the Highlands and the subsequent likelihood of rioting by aggrieved Northerners, the Government has decided to mix valium into the water supply of both Highland and Grampian Regions to calm the populace and lessen the chances of civil disorder. When asked by our staff if this was morally justifiable, a spokesman for Highland Regional Water PLC said today, "ZZZZZZZZ"

****

Last week's announcement from Cairngorm Chairlift Company of a new high tech funicular railway for their ski area had us all agog. Although the first shots have been fired in the conservation battle, this plan could push Speyside's ski-ing potential into the sci-fi domains of the next century. At the launch last week we were given a graphic illustration of the company's ease with modern technology. When a video monitor failed to work, the new General Manager Mr. Tim Whittome stepped forward smartly and gave it a hard slap. Presumably, minor tuning adjustments on the new uplift system will be done with a baseball bat. Several local worthies including many long serving workers in the ski business have been showing signs of pique at their exclusion from the guest list which numbered over 300. Good to know that the Aviemore

Health Centre doctors were all invited. Their contribution to the furthering of the local ski industry will undoubtedly be substantial. Readers are asked not to speculate on the reasons for their invitation especially regarding the expected scale of future injuries.

****

Recent talk about the need to have first-aiders present at shinty games reminds me that some years ago, one of our local medical men made a similar suggestion about Scottish Country Dances. In his opinion, if 'Strip the Willow' became much more popular, it could mean the end of the life as we know it. Leaving aside the usual bumps bruises and scratches more serious occurrences in the past weeks have included dislocated knee-caps and ruptured Achilles tendons. But could a first aider help those of us who have forsworn teetotalism in the interests of science, where Scottish country dancing hurts most? In the wallet (or sporran). These neatly uniformed and highly trained personnel, might rush in from the wings with massive injections of cash, transfusions of coinage and help in massaging the accounts while stopping your favourite correspondent from blowing things out of all proportion.

****

11

When Foolscap was just a single sheet before the days of marriage and children he used to like to slip away to a hotel for the weekend. A new angle on the short break holiday has been discovered at Holbeck Hall in Scarborough. You stay at home and the hotel slips away. As Holbeck Hall appears to have been a pleasant enough place to while away a weekend in the days before it slid gently into the sea it is felt that there are a number of more deserving local hotels that might have suffered this sinking feeling without depriving the nation of a decent hostelry. It would be churlish to name names but one can immediately think of several badly run eyesores that the earth could cheerfully swallow up without causing undue concern. The Foolscap staff are scouring the local area for suitably bad hotels and for a small bribe will happily keep 'shtum' about names and locations!

****

Trying to keep the price down department. This story reaches us from Carrbridge Councillor David Ritchie concerning a customer of his father Bob in the deep dark past.
A parsimonious crofter bent on home improvements approached him with this cautious specification.
" I don't want a proper window mind. I just want a pane o' glass wi' a bit wood round it that I can open and shut."

****

As a renowned arbiter of taste within the arts and literature, this column has rightly received an invitation for Monday the 12th at Struan House Hotel, Carrbridge to witness the release of the latest Album from The Brothers Gilly. This notorious singing and instrumental duo frequently pack Struan House on Monday nights; especially if they are playing at the Cairn! In spite of advice from this column the new album is not being entitled "A Kick in the Gillies" or "Caught By The Gillies" instead they have plumped for the more prosaic "Arrow Through My Heart". It contains 12 songs telling a story of two brothers playing in different areas of music for about twenty years brought together by strange circumstances (I wonder who they could be?) and is all self written and locally produced at Redwood Studios Carrbridge. The Brothers inform me that their highly individual style is a mixture of Cajun Celtic Rock And Pop which might well tempt some of our readers to refer to it by it's acronym.

****

The news that Frith Finlayson, the doyen of Scottish ski instructors and ex-owner of Ski School d'Ecosse is writing his memoirs has alarmed certain sections of Strathspey society. Frith who was one of the founders of BASI and a father of Scottish skiing has had a long and sometimes exciting life. Over the years he has been involved in a considerable amount of, what for the sake of propriety we will call, 'high jinks' some of which, we feel, must show up in the text of his autobiography. These are bound to include the names of his companions who may now feel that their

13

current respectability is somewhat at odds with their past history. Although no publisher has yet signed up the tome, a constant procession of furtive callers has been seen at the Finlayson door offering all sorts of inducements to halt publication. We understand that Frith is not willing to stifle his artistic ambitions for sordid cash. At least, not until they start talking sensible money!

****

The probity of the good Kingussie burghers has never been in any doubt however this story suggests that there are a number of opportunists among this damn fine body of men and women.
On the Monday immediately following the release of schoolchildren for the annual summer hols, the following was heard in the Kingussie branch of the Bank of Scotland whose customers are noted for their moral rectitude.
Small precocious child: "Did anybody drop a bundle of notes with an elastic band round it."
At this point the large queue of customers, patiently waiting to bank their ill gotten gains from the weekend, shouted as one man; "I did!"
Small precocious child: "Well I found the elastic band."

****

Because of the fear of highway robbery on the French roads the Automobile Association is issuing instructions to motorists to help them through the present difficulties. Foolscap, never the column to be left behind when advice is needed, has decided to issue some handy phrases which our readers may find useful if they are touring the continent and find themselves approached by felons. These phrases have been painstakingly translated word for word into French from many old Scottish sayings. Davie Johnstone of Inverdruie has suggested exclaiming "Au secours mon Robert" when approached. This of course means, 'Help ma bob.' He also suggests that once you are safely out of reach you could cry, "Votre tante culotte est tout hache de beouf," which is a derogatory expression currently popular in Glasgow meaning, 'Your knickers are all mince,' though just what it represents, I am unwilling to speculate. Any other readers with ideas for this series are welcome to contribute. Personally I would stick to simple exhortations such as; "Sur votre bicyclette, mon ami." 'On yer bike pal.' And when these modern day highwaymen discover that as an impoverished resident of Speyside you have nothing worth stealing; you can always exclaim, " Votre derriere est dehors la fenetre."

****

THE CASE OF THE SERIAL CLUBHOUSE BLAGGER.
After the break in at Grantown Golf Club on Saturday night, Carrbridge Golf Club suffered a similar incident on the following Monday night. Local Clubs are advised to be wary and especially security conscious while this arch-fiend is at liberty. The thief losing his nerve at the crucial moment only managed to get away with a box of Mars bars, a microwave oven and some golf balls from the Aladdin's cave that is Carrbridge Golf Clubhouse.

Immediately, there were highly coloured stories of someone going around local pubs trying to sell what he believed was a TV set, only to discover that the front opened every time he tried to switch it on. Police are said to be looking for a sweet-toothed, fast-food nut of low intelligence who had lost his balls.

****

When Foolscap is not bent over a hot word-processor or wiggling his quill, he can be an attentive and charming family man. In pursuing this side of his character he recently took his wife and progeny to the Highland Wildlife Park where the children, as pronounced a set of gargoyles as you are ever likely to meet, stared offensively at the animals. The youngest looking at a deer questions her mother.
"What kind of animal is that?"
"What do I call your dad every morning?"
hints Mrs Foolscap.
"Wowwee! I didn't know you could get
rats that big." responds the bratlet.

****

The following article came on the heels of a front page scoop which had told of a lady who had been accidentally locked in the public toilets in Grantown.

16

POETRY CORNER. Lounging around the 10th floor I cannot help thinking about my duty to bring culture to the masses and my mind immediately turns to poetry. As I have no sense of metre I generally warm towards the style of the late William Topaz McGonnagall. The front page story of last week's 'Strathie' supplied the necessary inspiration for my poetic gem:

> It was in the year nineteen hundred and ninety three,
> That a lady visitor to Grantown decided to go for a pee,
> While she was in, there was a terrible furore,
> So a woman from the council came along and locked the
>   door.
> The lady's husband became upset,
> "My wife has no' come oot from that toilet,"
> So he went to a nearby dentist to complain,
> Where the dentist said, "I feel no pain,"
> But nonetheless as a socially conscientious chap,
> He phoned the council office and thereby ended what might
>   easily have become a flap.
> Afterwards a spokesman named Mr. Henderson Pollock,
> Said, "I think we may have possibly dropped a clanger!"

****

17

The glorious twelfth passed not with a bang but with a whimper. In another column in another blatt I read of a Southern domiciled estate owner who phoned his ghillie in Scotland with the question, "How are the grouse?"
The ghillie replied,
"They're both fine."
Closer to home, our mole amongst the ghillies discusses the shortage of birds however he offers some sporting hope as he tells me,
"The hills o' Foregin is fair black wi' white hares".

****

Ian Malcolm the Chairperson of Aviemore Community Council and self styled Provost of Aviemore is currently holidaying at his summer residence, a cottage in the Provence area of France. As we read this he is officially meeting the Maire of this Clochemerle style village. Perhaps it is the time for Aviemore electors to consider erecting lamp-posts in front of his official residence in Dalfaber Road or perhaps setting up a public subscription to buy him a chain of office in order that he may assume the importance commensurate with his station. We may already be too late. Rumours are rife that before leaving for France he was in receipt of a communication from Aviemore Goldsmiths and Toilet Requisites Inc. regarding the acquisition of a length of ceremonial linkage. It is all too reminiscent of the old story of a local politico visiting some friends in England many years ago when a discussion on local government ensued.

"Do you have Mayors of your towns like we have?" asked the friend.

"Na na lad we hiv Proavosts, but they're mich the same."

"And tell me, do they wear chains?"

"Na na. We jist let them gang aboot free."

****

The Foolscap mole network is increasing. An Aviemore mole was interested to note curious goings-on at the Police Station there last week. The mole viewed three CID men pushing six trolley loads of beer and spirits up the ramp and in through the front door. I have heard of taking a case to court but six cases seems rather extravagant. Perhaps it is the first instalment for their Christmas party or maybe the Prisoners Aid Society has finally lost its grip on reality. Our mole, rather disappointingly, thought that it might be exhibit A in some criminal proceeding although it feared that the case, by the time it finally gets to court, might founder for lack of evidence. The most likely explanation must be that continuing the government's privatisation scheme and following Group 4's takeover of some prisons, we suspect that Scottish & Newcastle has made a successful bid for the Northern Constabulary.

****

One of our esteemed law lords, Lord Woolf in condemnation of the government's hard line stance on crime and punishment may seem to be on the right track but some of his ideas are rather advanced even for this column's enlightened if simple philosophy. One suggestion includes fining people who fail to protect their property and thus allow it to be burgled. This is not an entirely new concept. In olden time, Kings would sometimes kill the bearer of bad news, a policy which caused messengers to lose their enthusiasm for delivering such items. We suppose it follows, that while the perpetrators of crime are dealt with as humanely as possible, the victims should naturally be punished. In future anyone daring to go to the police to report a crime will first be fined and then beaten. This will have the desired effect of reducing reported crime figures to a record low. A more popular suggestion for improving the legal system is to retire judges before they go completely ga-ga.

****

My piece last month on Dentists has caused some re-action. A mole in Newtonmore phones the 10th floor to tell me of the current favourite joke in that village which is as follows;

What is the difference between the scene of a road accident involving a dentist and one involving a hedgehog?

There are skid marks in front of the hedgehog.

I realise that the popularity of dentists has never been high but their current policy seems to have dropped them to an all time low. Perhaps even below Estate Agents and Bank Managers. Heaven forbid.

1994

M rs Foolscap has decided that she is becoming something of a wit. She read in the Strathie a few weeks ago about the three policemen who were slightly injured in a car accident between Grantown and Aviemore. She thought the 'Police officers in crash' lacked inventiveness and should have been replaced with the simple but effective 'BOBBY CRUSH'. I don't like to encourage her so I said that she was giving her age away.

HISTORICAL NOTE: Bobby Crush was a popular musician of the seventies.

****

Still on the subject of ski-ing, (well I have to make the most of it while we have snow) a fan hands me a cutting of an article on Scottish Ski-ing culled from the normally erudite columns of the Sunday Times Scotland dated 2nd January. The author of the piece, who I will not embarrass by naming, discusses the chairlift company's proposed funicular train set as follows:

22

"At the Cairngorms ski centre near Aviemore, a £15m expansion is under way. Work on Britain's first vernacular railway to take skiers up the mountain will begin next year."
After much earnest discussion at the Foolscap think tank we have to presume that a vernacular railway is one that is only being talked about.

****

This column scans the world's press to bring interesting stories to its readers and also to while away the hours in its luxurious suite of rooms on the 10th floor at Strathie Tower. In the course of this study we came across the following piece of news regarding the Sultan of Brunei. With his entourage numbering twenty people the Sultan, arguably the world's richest man with an estimated fortune of around £40 billion give or take a billion or two, went shopping in New York. After a short browse in a well known store he picked a bauble costing 60,000 dollars and offered his American Express card in payment. The assistant explained that in purchases of this size, extra identification was required. The Sultan as a Head of State carries no passport and was temporarily stumped till a member of his staff fished out a Brunei banknote and asked the assistant to compare the picture on the note with the gentleman at the counter. After a few moments silent study of the banknote the assistant said, "That'll do nicely."

****

FOOLSCAP BROUGHT TO BOOK ──────────────

*Occasionally in order to combat the rise of poetry in the valley, Foolscap
has had to resort to taking up the pen himself.*

POETRY CORNER   Who says I cannot push back the frontiers
of artistic enlightenment in Strathspey? After recent frightening
poetic experiences in this paper I am persevering manfully. Here
on the 10th floor we are sensible that next Tuesday, Jan 25th, is
Burns' night and in honour of the bard we unearthed a yellowing
piece of paper from the back of a drawer in the leather topped
Sheraton desk. On it was written the following:

TO A POSTIE (Not a particular Postie, just any Postie)
by a friend of Robert Burns

Wee sleekit cowrin timorous postie
O, Tak' yer time and eat a toastie
Thou shouldna start awa sae hastie
            Wi' rattle 'n' jerk.
Hae yersel a decent breakfast
            Afore yer work.

Ye dash aboot through Grantown streets
Then out to see the farmland treats
Fleein' by the sheep and pigs
            Upon the roonds
Workin' hard and stayin' sober
            Tae earn yer poonds.

I'm truly sorry Man's Dominion
Has upset Grantown Mothers' Union
They fight like mad for votes for women
And jobs like yours
They havena' a hope and fine they know it
The silly things.

But postie thou art no thy lane
The job they want is jist my ain
Our lives are but a constant struggle
Wi' oot much pay
The best laid schemes of poets and posties
Gang aft a-gley.

From verses such as these, old Scotia's grandeur springs. It is obviously very moving. Reading it aloud to our editor Ken Smith, I noticed him discreetly dab at his eyes with a handkerchief throughout.

****

Meribel-Mottaret, France. Allo, allo. Vous probably pensed that vous would jamais hear from moi again. Mais vous etes mistaken because ici je am. It is I, Foolscap. You see me suitably attired sunning myself on the slopes here on the roof of the world. The hotel is at around 6000ft so breathing can be difficult especially when my room mate has a pillow over my face to stop me snoring. Travelling, I have had to rub shoulders with the common man.

25

The common man nowadays is a middle class baby boomer, probably an accountant, who is married with two point four children the point fourth being by far the worst behaved. I am sorry to say that the common man is a complete pain in the neck. They talk to each other loudly with references to their lifestyle in the forlorn hope of impressing us mere peasants. I find myself staring malevolently at each in turn until they become uncomfortable and shut up. This light entertainment helps to pass the journey.

The ski-ing makes up for the journey. Fresh snow every night gives conditions that are superb. Two of the days we encounter conditions that are reminiscent of Cairngorm at its worst. Always worth remembering that it can happen in the Alps too! These minor setbacks mean nothing to we Scottish Calvinists who find it quite pleasant to have high winds, nil visibility and frostbite after all the sun on the first three days. It is possible that I may just decide to stay and send my jottings to Strathie Tower from my palatial apartments here.

****

Home again on the tenth floor proving that I didn't decide to stay and the gossip starts flowing already as the following bucolic tale shows. Local keepers have a trying and exhausting life, crawling through the heather and hauling ex-Stags down hillsides. Nowadays thing are easier for them since they have acquired Land Rovers, Argocats and even lorries to ease their burdens.

After a day's shooting when all the gentlemen guests had left, Reidhaven head keeper Frank Law of Inverlaidnan was being assisted by a young student while loading the kill onto a truck. The last beast was a particularly large and heavy one. "Grab the hind legs and we'll swing him onto the back of the lorry," cries Frank. The young man struggles with the oversized Stag and they have a couple of failed attempts. "He's an awkward one this," pants the young student. "Well, y'see," says Frank thoughtfully, "he's probably never been on a lorry before."

****

According to an informant in Cromdale, it is only the female cucumber that gives us indigestion. Sufferers from stomach ailments will be anxious to identify the differences between the sexes in order to avoid digestive disorders. Working purely on guesswork this column assumes that it has only ever seen male cucumbers and in fact is unsure what a female cucumber might look like. Readers who wish to send in suggestions about the appearance of this succulent are welcome to do so but should take care not to breach the normally high standards of decency, correctness and morality for which this column is justly renowned.

****

MANCHESTER, ENGLAND. This column goes to enormous lengths to broaden the horizons of its readership. Here it is on another fact finding tour, this time to the rain capital of England. The police here tell me that there is a car stolen in Manchester every six minutes. All I can say is that the owner must be incredibly careless. He should give up cars and use the trams. The city now supports a new tram service, opened in 1992, using tracks set into the streets around the city centre and disused railway tracks elsewhere. From the point of view of it's passengers it offers a brisk and efficient metro system although in the centre of town the motorists competing for road space may not agree. Investigating this phenomenon on your behalf I use the trams to go about my business. Eventually I am forced to conclude that they have little application in the Highlands so, stopping only long enough to fill out my expenses sheet, I set off for home.

****

It is always comforting to know that the educational system is preparing the young of the country for their brave new world. At a time when we are entering into full partnership in the European Community, Grantown Grammar School is cutting its language department. No longer can apt second year pupils elect to take French and German. From now on they can only take one of these however they are offered two choices of Home Economics in their course options. In the next century Grantown youngsters will be well prepared to compete in the business world with their European counterparts. When it comes to thrashing out the nitty

gritty in commercial or political
debate they may not be able to
speak the language but they
will still have the chance to
make their presence felt by
throwing home made buns.

****

The Cairngorm Recreational Trust Ltd. has a new secretary. The 'old board', as it is known, oversees the affairs of Cairngorm Chairlift Co Ltd for reasons which have never been adequately explained although how this unwieldy group, it has approximately 70 members, can ever achieve anything is one of the great mysteries of the world. The new secretary is to be Sandy Caird whose penny-pinching talents are widely revered and it is felt that his influence may manifest itself in a variety of different ways. Suggestions so far include: Pay-as-you-go toilets, wind generated electricity and child slave labour. He could, of course, generate an immediate income of a around £15000 by asking all the board members to pay for their free season tickets.

****

Continuing with our series of bucolic tales we hear tell of a story about a tourist wandering the back roads around Cromdale when he comes upon a small girl walking with a bull, leading it by the ring in its nose. The tourist somewhat taken aback at the disparity in size between the two says to the small child,

"Where are you going with that bull?"

"I'm taking it up to the cows in the top field," replies the girl.

"Surely," says the shocked tourist, "that's a job for your father."

"No," replies the girl, "It's got to be the bull."

****

April 1st, or All Fool's Day as it is sometimes known, is a day which is close to this column's heart for one reason or another. This year brought the usual crop of silliness and trickery which we have all come to expect. Some wag at Cairngorm Chairlift put up a sign reading "CRASH HELMETS MUST BE WORN ON THE FUNICULAR." Various local persons who shall remain nameless but who should have known better asked where the funicular was. The chairlift company who at first showed some displeasure against the unknown perpetrator were later mollified on discovering that their ski rental department had hired out ten crash helmets. This festival of foolishness is always open to misunderstanding and the following story attests to this fact. The manager of the Dalfaber Golf & country club, Jonathan Gatenby, chose that fateful morning to chop some sticks at his Newtonmore home. With the natural accuracy and attention to detail which he brings to all his dealings, Jonathan managed to strike his thumb with the axe, a feat which resulted in a lot of noise and a pool of blood in the garden. He quickly phoned an acquaintance to ask

30

for assistance but found that April Fools Day is not the best day to make requests of this nature. After the phone had been put down on him three times by a suspicious and paranoid friend, he gave up and drove himself to hospital with one hand. Now that he is almost fully recovered he can devote his spare time to cleaning the bloodstains from the car upholstery.

****

Bill Mitchell (the ex-sea dog not the golfer) has been wisely missing his evening pint while waiting for his nephew to re-plumb his two year old house. It does not pay to come rolling home with a full bladder to find the toilet out in the hall and a nephew's head sticking up through the floorboards. Bill, whose parsimony is renowned in all the pubs in Grantown, has amused his friends greatly with constant complaints about the enormous appetite of this young sanitary engineer. Just what was wrong with the almost new original plumbing is unknown but we must presume that it did not come up to nautical specifications. No doubt he will be anxious to have all work complete before brother Don arrives to sponsor the Madeira Cup once more. The competition will be played this Saturday at Grantown Golf Club and will include some local players and a group of dubious timeshare salesmen from Madeira. A brief note to the local lads. Don't take your cheque-books with you and don't sign anything except your bar bill.

****

31

Bucolic Tales 3: A West Coast crofter is leaning over the fence watching his sheepdog play as a tourist walks past.

"Good day" says the tourist. The crofter taking the pipe from his mouth replies with a Gaelic greeting.

"Aha," says our tourist friend, "you are speaking in your native tongue."

"D'ye have the Gaelic yersel'?" asks the crofter.

"I don't speak it but I understand it," claims the tourist cautiously.

"My goodness, isn't that the coincidence," responds the crofter, "that dog of mine there is chust the same."

****

Grantown Grammar's very own folk group, Frostbite, has been invited to travel to Denmark. The group performed for a visiting party of Danish head teachers who were so impressed that they invited them back to their country to give a series of concerts. The generous hearted Danes offered to supply all accommodation and food for the party provided that they could transport themselves to Denmark. This meant raising about £150 each which they planned to do by the usual methods: raffles, teas, sponsored whatnots and pleading with generous local institutions. The Danish Education Authority surprised them with an added donation of £500 towards their travel. Fired with enthusiasm and confidence from this burst of largesse they approached Highland Region Education Dept who offered them exactly £500 less than the Danes. Zilch.

Apocryphal Stories No. 4: A lady placed an advert in the deaths column of a well known Aberdeen Journal. The Editor, a man of the finest sensibilities, was horrified to read the line which said simply. "Jimmy Reid frae Peterheid is deid." He rushed after the woman to tell her that this wouldn't do. "But it's all I can afford," she replied. The Editor not only a man of the finest sensibilities but a man with a kind heart said to the girl at the desk, "Let this lady have an extra three words free of charge." The following day, swiftly reading the deaths column to check the result of his generosity he was shocked to find: "Jimmy Reid frae Peterheid is deid; Volkswagen for sale."

****

This column has no desire to take the bread out of other columnists mouths or indeed to poach on another's preserve however at the risk of upsetting Cameron MacNeish, seen at large further down this page, this column heaved its twelve and a half stone up Carn Eilrig on Saturday in the company of two of its moles. The smaller and fitter mole irritated the two heavier and less trim members by trotting up the steepest bits apparently unconcerned. Had this column found the breath to catch him up it would have kicked him squarely in his map pocket. Always supposing it could find the energy. At the top, a mere 2500 feet we had our meagre lunch in the mandatory howling gale and admired the scenery. From this unique vantage point we could see Loch Einich where our water comes from, Aviemore, Loch Morlich, Cairngorm and the Lairig Ghru. Our knees are still sore from the effort and our lungs nearly burst getting to the top. Later that day while we were recovering in a licensed premises, local wit and raconteur Hugh Clark in an uncharacteristic burst of benevolence suggested that perhaps the views had taken our breath away.

****

Impatient watchers of the progress of Aviemore's new village green will have noticed a death defying skateboard ramp being constructed last week. Many assumed that this was another cunning plan from the fertile imagination of Ron Stuart now widely known as the district's Detrimental Officer. Skateboarding enthusiasts amongst us will have been disappointed to note that almost as soon as it was completed, it was demolished and replaced with a more gentle slope so that it might fulfil a more suitable role as a wheelchair access. Being naturally cynical we on the 10th floor can't help wondering who will end up paying for this. The new railings have been greatly admired by one and all and a number of the high spirited are waiting for targets to be painted on the large round metal discs which adorn the tops so that they can take a better aim. Although the sign saying "completion Easter 1994" has been removed I have been assured by a spokesperson that the green will still be completed by Easter ... but not necessarily 1994.

****

34

Lady Pauline, who is intending soon to open her estate, Craig Revack, to an unsuspecting public is also noted for her dedication to the estate of marriage. Indeed her enthusiasm for that marital institution rivals many Hollywood movie stars. At the recent reopening of the new improved Cromdale hall revellers could not ignore the two plaques. The first read "Opened by Lady Pauline Ogilvy-Sykes in 1965" whilst on the other side the latest plaque read "Opened by Lady Pauline Nicholson in 1994." The question on everyone's lips was: "What happened to all the other commemorative plaques in between."

****

A local lady stood in her garden with her four year old grandson looking at a dead mole. As a group, four year old boys are not the most sympathetic when considering the concept of death. "It's sad." said Granny. The Grandson replied: "No it isn't, it's dead."

****

With the hurly burly of the European elections now past we should spare a thought for those poor souls who stood and failed. What have they lost. Substantial salaries, which for British representatives amount to a mere £42,000 per annum. They also get a pay-off equivalent to 16 months salary if they retire or are voted out. Lest you should be worried that they might find it difficult to survive on this niggardly amount have no fear. The expenses are extremely generous and are said to be almost bottomless like the everlasting bottle of Guinness. Being an MEP is the next best thing to being a multi millionaire; almost impossible to run out of money. In the best traditions of democracy we are prepared to give it a try. Following the philosophy of Screaming Lord Sutch and his Monster Raving Loony Party, the 10th floor has now become the headquarters of the 'Foolscap Give Us A Leg Up Onto The Gravy Train And Watch Us Go' party. At the next Euro Elections we plan to field candidates in all the Scottish seats in the hope of securing a sound basis for the Foolscap fortune. With the rise of the SNP and the threat of independence one step closer, I will need a considerable sum to further progress my claim to the throne of Scotland.

✻✻✻✻✻✻✻✻✻✻✻✻✻✻✻✻✻

Some weeks ago this column made some remarks about old sea-dog Bill Mitchell's caution when opening his wallet and also to the problems encountered while re-plumbing his house. Captain Billy, as he is sometimes known, is a man with literary leanings and has responded in rhyme in the style of Kipling. Not the one who makes the cakes; the one what wrote the poems:

If (with apologies to Rudyard Kipling)

If you can keep your head when all about you
Are slagging you and laughing fit to bust.
If you can plot revenge while seeming not to,
Reviled by chaps you once thought you could trust.

If you are made the butt (with so called humour)
Of some appalling hack's acidic wit,
Or the subject of some vile and baseless rumour
Just serve the b***** with another writ.

If you can smile at jokes about your dunny
And strive to keep your cool while this same hack
Makes cracks about your shrewd regard for money
(Now he'll never get the pint, that's owed him, back.)

If you can bear this sly persistent knocking
Be stoic tho' the jeers may scandalise
And being mocked at, don't give way to mocking
But break his legs with friendship in your eyes.

If you can fill the unforgiving minute
With every dirty trick beneath the sun,
Yours is the Earth and everything that's in it,
And, what is more, you'll be a journalist you bum.

****

Kyle of Lochalsh. Wester Ross. Great things are happening in
this small West Coast port with the construction of the new toll
bridge to the Isle of Skye. Many local people think that the
bridge will dramatically affect their lives and in at least one area
this looks like being the case. A few years ago Highland Region
decided to upgrade the toilet facilities near the ferry slip and built

37

a super loo similar to the one in Aviemore and demanded a similar entry fee. At around the same time the ferry company, Caledonian MacBrayne, stopped charging for foot passengers and now charge only for cars making the three minute crossing. Rather than pay for the privilege of spending a penny, parsimonious locals with time on their hands now take the short crossing and use the toilet facilities on the ferry free of charge. There are strong rumours that the ferry company is shortly to change it's name to pee & owe.

****

Still in Wester Ross I hear the following story of a thirty-something married couple going out to dine at Dornie for a birthday celebration. As is the way on these occasions the husband part of the team drank more than was absolutely necessary while the wife member stayed reasonably sober. At home the husband struggled out of his party suit and into his bed where amorous ambitions overtook him. Full of hope he tenderly caressed his partner. In a withering tone she said, "It's my birthday not yours!" then turned over and went to sleep.

****

We seem to be a nation of toast eaters so it is surprising that for a simple enough concept the pop-up toaster has baffled the best brains and the largest and most powerful electrical goods companies in the world. It is impossible to buy a toaster at any price that actually does the job for which it was intended. This column once owned a very cheap toaster which successfully completed each mission but since it died after having a knife poked in it to dislodge a stuck piece of toast no other toaster has accomplished what should be a simple task. Some do one side only, some manage to leave a white ribbon along one edge, some burn the edges but leave the middle white while others cannot be relied upon to toast to the same degree twice in a row. Our most recent acquisition has so far accomplished all of these. On the face of it there shouldn't be any problem. The concept seems simple enough for a society that can put a man on the moon and can make stripey toothpaste.

****

Residents of Speyside are themselves also tourists and at this time of year those not actively engaged in the tourist business like to get away to meet new civilisations and to boldly go across the channel. Holidays wouldn't be the same without a little drama or disappointment. Duncan Grant a leading thespian and stalwart of Grantown Drama Club went to the Dordogne. To save currency he decided to use his flexible friend and travelled right down to the Dordogne and back using his little plastic card for everything. It was refused only once. When they stopped for their last holiday meal. Fifteen miles from home at a fast food restaurant very close to Aviemore railway station! As many of you will have read in a previous edition, our editor Ken Smith also drove single handed to the Dordogne without major incident. What he failed to mention in his glowing published report was that he got lost in Glasgow on the way home. However we save our greatest sympathy for the head of Grantown Grammar P.E department, Ronnie Mathieson. 'Bonnie' Ronnie as he is unaccountably known was relaxing in a villa in Spain when he discovered that his car had been clamped. The little misunderstandings which so often creep into dealings with foreign policemen resulted in 'Bonnie' Ronnie doing a short stretch of Spanish porridge in the local nick. Sadly this meant that Mr. Mathieson, who is a byword for sartorial style, may have a slightly striped effect to his sun tan and we shudder to think what he looked like in a serge suit covered in little arrows.

****

An exasperated housewife in the Co-op in Grantown was overheard talking to her friend. "I'm not buying bananas any more. They just eat them." This remark leaves us with the worrying question of what Grantonians normally do with bananas.

****

The Grantown Show comes around yet again with its subtle blend of the bucolic life and the excitement of Terminator 2. This year's show was technically the best ever in spite of the announcer omitting to mention our MEP Mrs Winnie Ewing in the list of dignitaries present. The various stands offering refreshments were crammed with people many of whom wouldn't know a tractor from a Clydesdale and certainly couldn't tell them apart by the time they left. With the income from their exorbitant charges the banks were able to offer unprecedented levels of hospitality to the great and the good excepting, of course, the poor souls such as Foolscap who contribute so much to their profits. The highlight of the day was seeing our lovable editor Ken Smith being sexually harassed by the Abernethy WRI ladies as he attempted to leave. After winning a romantic evening for two and the Drumdunan cup, the ladies, unable to contain their excitement, were celebrating uproariously on a travelling rug in the car park with a bottle of wine.

****

The 'No Nonsense' Agency run by itinerant bearded and kilted folk singer Duncan Stewart better known by his sound-alike soubriquet, 'drunken stupor', has joined the growing band of Aviemore businesses using a mobile phone. Should we suddenly find ourselves in dire need of an emergency folk singer at two o'clock in the morning we will know just who to ring. In Duncan's case the acquisition of this new toy may well be excusable as he is himself equally mobile, seldom in the same location twice with the possible exception of the Old Bridge Inn. In spite of the cellphone it is difficult to describe Duncan as a yuppie and even more difficult to classify him at all. The new agency whose full name is No Nonsense Agency For Entertainers will have the interesting and, no doubt, accurate acronym NNAF Entertainers. Regarding the bold impresario's invariable garb of shirt and kilt we were at a loss to discover where the offending portable was carried until we noticed the bulge in his sporran. This, no doubt, has the added advantage of impressing his enormous band of female fans.

****

Charlie 'Spar', Grantown's answer to Fortnum & Mason, certainly knows his way about a shop however there is strong evidence that outside his own premises his orienteering skills may leave a little to be desired. Being the good samaritan that he undoubtedly is, Charlie took a stranded grouse plucker (No! Sorry fans! Not a pheasant plucker) to Speyside's latest tourist attraction, Revack Estate. Unfamiliar with the new road system within the estate Charlie kept on along what he assumed was the right track. The track went further and got rougher in equal proportions until the unfortunate pair ended up stuck in a ditch. Poor Charlie was obliged to walk ignominiously back to the lodge and fetch a keeper with a Land Rover, who pulled him out. Perhaps he should give up the life of a back-woodsman and stick to the shop.

****

The long awaited planning application for Cairngorm Chairlift Company's new Funny-peculiar Railway is greeted with different emotions in different places. Here on the 10th floor we have several important concerns. When the railway is completed and starts operating, will it be closed down by strike action every Tuesday and Wednesday? It may be that with a new chairman about to be elected, this might be a good time to invite Jimmy Knapp to join the board. Are we to assume that the clear felling around the Glenmore area is simply to build up stocks for a wood burning funicular which might be sponsored by the Strathspey Steam Railway. Lastly, who is going to start the whip round to buy a top hat for the company's present Chairman, Harry Brown, so that he can slip more comfortably into his role as the Fat Controller.

****

There was some acrimonious debate surrounding the funding of new bowling greens when existing greens were thought to be under utilised. This prompted the following cartoon.

"NICE OF KINGUSSIE BOWLING CLUB TO SEND US NEW BOWLS AS A GOODWILL GESTURE !"

****

The marble and gold telephone on my ornate Sheraton desk gives a discreet ring. A voice says "Hold the front page." It turns out to be Ian Malcolm self-styled Provost of Aviemore trying to make a little extra holiday money as one of my moles, before departing for his bijou hideaway home in Provence. Apparently that doyen of the Scottish ski trade, climber hillwalker and ex-rugby star of the London Scottish, Sandy Caird, has suffered a dramatic ski style injury in one of the hottest and driest summers for many years. He has broken his leg. Just what dangerous sport, in which exotic location, caused this I hear you ask? Not glacier ski-ing nor climbing the Matterhorn. Sandy was just walking off the first tee at Nethybridge Golf Course when he caught his foot in a rabbit hole and fell. No doubt, as soon as he is released from Raigmore, he will be contacting ski specialists Salomon to suggest a new product. Safety release golf shoes.

****

As many of our well travelled readers will know, Nethybridge nowadays likes to call itself the forest village which it does with justifiable pride. It would be embarrassing for the good villagers if I was to spill the beans that for their recent Highland Games they were obliged to import a Caber from Newtonmore. Rather than cause any discord I will keep my lips sealed. No one need ever know.

****

In a recent conversation with a member of the Northern Constabulary I discover that the Crime Prevention department has changed to the Crime Management department. We must presume that because they have had little success at preventing crime, they have decided to manage it instead. Can we assume that henceforth the Chief Constable will be known simply as 'Mr. Big' and is it fair to expect that the Northern Constabulary is going to be the first government department to show a profit? It will certainly mean that the complications of working out the rota will be a lot easier. The crooks and the cops can all have the same days off.

****

It was a great pleasure to hear that the recent Council Meeting in Kingussie resounded with enormous hilarity. In an early exchange our fresh faced reporter Paul Hunter scored well when Councillor Cameron made unkind remarks about this blatt. After Davie's remarks had brought about the first round of laughter he apologised to our man with the words "Sorry Paul." Our quick witted man of action replied, "You will be Davie." which caused a second titter to run around the table. The high spot of the day, however, came later when Vice Chair Tom Wade was discussing his meeting with Scotrail and the possibility of restricting sleeper services on the Perth Inverness line. Councillor Stuart Black regaled the meeting, to bellowing guffaws, with tales of his wedding night in one of British Rail's sleeping compartments. Unfortunately, because of his mirth, our man neglected to note down the details for this column.

Last week's Strathie carried a once in a lifetime ad in the situations vacant column. It cannot be often that this illustrious organ carries an advert for a RADIO BROADCASTER. It turns out that Cairngorm Chairlift Co. are looking for just such a person. This sounds like just the job for Foolscap with his wit, wisdom and intimate knowledge of the ski industry. (What's that white stuff called?) However after considering the company's future plans to build a funny peculiar railway, we may be able to explain the job more clearly. To do so I have managed to get hold of the kids' crayons and create another cartoon masterpiece for the delight of the readers. (Not, - Ed.).

****

Your favourite columnist is obliged to travel the length and breadth of Scotland seeking out new civilisations and boldly going where no man has gone before. In my travels I recently visited the office in Kyle of Lochalsh which dispenses information on the new bridge to Skye, currently in an advanced state of construction. The road from the South and East which connects with the bridge passes close by Kyle Golf Club, a previously secluded spot with an awkward access. Generously the construction company suggested a scheme to build a short connecting road to replace the existing narrow, tortuous track. At this point the authorities discovered that the area was the habitat of a group of otters and banned further development. Local humorists, after exposure to the large number of German tourists who visited the area this summer, are now referring to the road as the 'Otterban.'

****

Glaswegians have a curious sense of humour at times especially where sheep and the highlands are concerned, however we hear that these citizens have re-named the popular film 'Silence of the Lambs.' They call it 'Shut up Ewes.!'

****

Bowlers, it would seem, are a funny lot. Hot on the heels of the acrimonious debate over the new Carrbridge bowling green, we hear now that the Aviemore bowlers don't wish to be associated with the proposed new Aviemore Community Sports Centre. This publicly funded centre is to include a swimming pool, day care services and multifarious sports and is seen as a replacement for the village hall. The bowlers however wish to practise their arts in secret and are now looking independently at a site in Burnside where, by a strange happenstance, the Royal Observer Corps underground bunker is situated. This sounds like the ideal location for Aviemore's secretive bowlers. They could have their clubhouse in the ex ROC control room far from the prying eyes of squash players, swimmers, toddlers and other similarly dangerous citizens. It is fifty feet below ground.

1995

Two young gentlemen from a distant place far to the South found themselves travelling through darkest Aberdeenshire and decided, as young men will, to stop for a minor refreshment at a licensed establishment. "Do you have any real ale?" they enquired of the ample Buchan lady behind the bar. "Ahinna," she replied economically. The two lads considered this for a moment before placing their order. "OK gives us two whiskies and two half pints of Ahinna."

****

Readers will be aware of recent scandals in the press regarding footballers and their capacity for earning vast sums of money. Sometimes they earn much for playing well but if the dailies are to be believed, the benefits can be far greater for playing badly. A letter, addressed to Fool Scap on the 10th floor, from Will MacKean of the Haugh Hotel in Cromdale has just been discovered under a pile of empty beer bottles. It begins:
Dear Mr. Scap, and then maunders on about the situation before getting to the nub.

"Last season I had the dubious honour to be the goalie for

Cromdale F.C. The records show that without a shadow of doubt I was the least efficient keeper in the league. Luckily, perhaps through drink, or maybe old age, my memory will not reveal exactly how many goals I conceded.

Now, the Public Bar of the Haugh is, at times, a hotbed of rumour and animated discussion. Of late I have heard talk of "bungs" and "doing a Brucie". No one has yet accused me outright but it is surely only a matter of time. I would like to get my defensive tackle in first, something that the Cromdale team were so often incapable of doing last season.

For the record, I would categorically state that I received not a penny for any of the goals I conceded last season. All I got was the cheers of the opposition and the abuse of my team-mates. If the finger of suspicion need be pointed in any direction, perhaps the Manager of the Club might become nervous. It was he who selected me for the team, sure in the knowledge that a clean sheet was a remote possibility. It is he who is building a huge mansion in the village, not I."

It would seem that Cromdale is a seething caldron of corruption, rumour and innuendo and the sort of place that Bishop Heber must have had in mind when he wrote, "Though every prospect pleases, and only man is vile."

I think Foolscap will have to go there for a pint sometime soon.

****

My Aviemore mole sends me an apocryphal story regarding a member of the Cairngorm Chairlift Company staff who was asked to measure the height of a flagpole. Sometime after the instruction was issued a colleague spotted him trying to climb the pole to get the measurement and, with the best of intentions, suggested that it would be easier if the flagpole was lowered and laid flat on the ground. At this point the pole climber is said to have replied vociferously, "That's no good. I don't want the length of it, I want the height!"

****

The world's favourite columnist (yes, with hundreds of copies of the Strathie going to the US, Canada, Australia and dozens going to almost every country under the sun or under the snow, including one copy to Moscow [how's it going Leonid?] the Strathie is becoming a truly international newspaper) has spent many years laughing at the misfortunes of others and parading their hard luck stories in public. Sad to say that retribution has been visited upon Foolscap. As the last edition of this column was hitting the streets (if the Strathie can be said to hit the streets) I was ski-ing down Cairngorm in the company of Aviemore's Provost Malcolm when I fell on my pole hara kiri style, narrowly missing a ritual disembowelling, but managing, nonetheless, to dislocate my right shoulder. After several amusing attempts to replace it during which your favourite columnist showed himself in his true colours and screamed for mercy, I was despatched to Raigmore. Here after taking my wimpish nature into account they wisely laid me out completely before attempting further mauling. I have been ordered to keep this arm completely immobilised for at least two weeks which as I am right handed means that I cannot drive, write, pick my nose or wipe my bum. I have had several offers of help with the first two but as yet the other two are proving difficult to sell. All right you victims of Foolscap. Laugh!

****

Returning briefly to skiing and international recognition, shortly before my unfortunate accident (you won't get any more sympathy - Ed.)[I couldn't get any less, - flscp.] a photographer from a Swedish newspaper persuaded your favourite columnist to ski in a kilt and expose his knees (lets hope it was only his knees - Ed.) to the great Swedish public. I stood heroically gazing into the rising sun then cut a dash whizzing down amongst the baffled groups of skiers in the interests of promoting the area to the Swedes. The 10th floor is now preparing itself for the inevitable flood of fan mail, from pouting scandinavian blondes, which must start pouring in soon.

****

Watching Channel 4 the other night I was horrified to see the familiar features of Cameron McNeish who, as a few of you must have noticed, also writes for this blatt. Cameron is the presenter of the programme on the Great Outdoors and, as his reader will know, has been writing for the Strathie over many years. He

52

does not, of course, have access to my luxurious suite of rooms up here on the 10th floor of Strathie Tower as this sort of extravagance is reserved for those touched with genius such as myself and editor Ken Smith whose own suite on the 11th floor rivals even my own for sumptuousness. The McNeish entry to the world of television and its concomitant fame will have him surrounded soon by screaming fans demanding a lock from his already meagre supply of hair. It must also surely augur well for my own career. It means that the Strathie is the obvious starting point for a life in the heady world of television. Can it be long before the 'Foolscap' show is networked on every channel in Britain? After that; the world. A word of caution. Cameron has been writing here for at least 15 years longer than I, so, readers should keep their eyes peeled somewhere around the year 2010 for my entry to super-stardom.

****

Hard Luck Section: Youthful, athletic Ian Turner, Manager of the Mercury Hotel in Aviemore, is wont to join his colleagues for a weekly meeting when they are able to discuss matters of great weight and moment. Last week Ian, who feels stuck in a rut in which his wife always seems to have the car, phoned for a taxi to take him the half mile or so to his gossip session. The taxi arrived and tooted so Ian sprinted out to the hotel car park almost running straight into his own car parked therein. Aha. It was his turn to have the car. Not having the heart to cancel the waiting taxi or the courage to admit his mistake, he meekly got in and was driven to the meeting. After this extravagance he was unwilling to fritter any more money on transport and was obliged to walk back to work.

****

That harbinger of Spring, the dreaded 'Car Boot Sale' has already started to rear its ugly head (or to be more accurate; its ugly boot) once more. Whilst we are always happy to view the changing seasons from our lofty position up here on the 10th floor of Strathie Tower, the onset of the car boot sale brings a sense of depression, and futility causing the think tank (two floors below) once more to question the reason for life, the universe and fate itself. At the first example of the genre my mole spies well known Grantown thespian (they can't touch you for it) Bill Quirie surrounded by curious artefacts which must surely represent a substantial part of his personal history. Amongst a number of interesting items such as a Wendy House and a trampoline my mole sees an old leather saddle with a broken girth. As the Quirie household owns no horse, except perhaps for a clothes horse, speculation is now rife among the less respectable minds in Grantown as to the previous use of this article, some going as far as to suggest that the trampoline may well have been implicated. Any readers who feel that they may be able to supply the answer are advised to keep it strictly to themselves.

****

Grantown Golf Club's recent shotgun foursome was once again won by the usual team of Willie Lawson, Davie Fergusson, George Bain and Gordon Grant. As this is the fourth time in succession that they have carried away this particular prize dark mutterings were heard amid which calls came for a Dope Test. It was established quickly that a Dope test is something that this particular team would pass with flying colours. Another cry went up. "What about a urine test?" " No problems," cried the winning team, "We'll get it in the bottle every time."

****

And lastly from the department of WE KNOW WHAT THEY MEAN comes the tale of the local Welfare league match between Boat of Garten and Kingussie. Malcolm Taylor of Boat warning a fellow defender to mark a Kingussie opponent was heard offering the following advice. "You'll need to watch him like glue." Whilst Boat went on to lose 0-9 they stayed ahead on mixed metaphors.

****

Further on the subject of policepersons, the persons concerned were recently polled nationally on the thorny subject of carrying guns which I am glad to say they have voted against with a massive majority of 79%. In spite of this democratic drubbing, a few of the policepersons are still in favour of permanent arming so for them we repeat this poignant and cautionary tale heard on Radio 2 but originating, naturally, in the USA where gun toting cops are

55

the norm:

Police were called to an incident on a bridge where a young man was threatening suicide. When the officers arrived, they carefully and painstakingly talked to the young man. Their training in this sort of thing coupled with kindness and consideration was such that they eventually persuaded him not to jump and tenderly helped him over the barrier to safety. At this point the young man made a sudden movement, searching for something on his person, and one of the officers mistakenly believed that he was drawing a gun. Sadly for the recently saved soul, he was shot dead by his rescuers.

****

The unusually hot spell has forced some changes in the executive suites at the top of Strathie Tower. While writing, I am reclining naked in the cool breeze from the air-conditioning, my modesty only at risk from passing helicopters. The jacuzzi has been filled with ice cubes and the plumbing of my ornate fountain has been re-routed through a beer cooler to help keep the atmosphere bearable but in spite of all these precautions the last glass of champagne tasted distinctly tepid. I move to the window, first  putting on my hat in case anyone is watching. Outside the valley of the Spey is spread out before me bathed in equatorial sunshine and the local populace is sunbathing fit to burst. The unseasonal sight of gritters moving around our roads is perhaps not entirely unheard of even in June but on this occasion these machines are being used all over the Highland Region uniquely to spread sand on the melting road surface rather than their more usual pursuits. Readers need not panic. No doubt by the time you read this we will, once more, be enjoying torrential rain and near zero temperatures.

****

Achiltibuie. I am reclining on a sun kissed beach roughly the size of Grantown along with only a handful of people. Where else could we experience such peace and tranquillity blended with dramatic scenery. The weather is an unusual bonus. The beach at Achnahaird is a few miles from Achiltibuie and in the shadow of Stac Pollaidh and Suilven. The only drawback to what might seem an idyllic life is that I am obliged to share a small caravan with the Foolscap children which makes the Black Hole of Calcutta seem like a bit of a dawdle by comparison. Still enjoying the benefits of the continuing heatwave, the other major advantage in my being miles away to the West was missing the sight of a well-known Dorback farmer who was spotted driving his tractor wearing nothing more than a smile and a pair of espadrilles. The disturbing mental picture which this conjures up has almost put me off my beer.

The Boat Gala last weekend, was the usual social success but was not without incident. The brave lads of the Aviemore Fire Brigade (Motto-"Keep it going and we'll be along in a minute.") were out in force as is their public spirited wont for such charitably inclined occasions. Under their Captain Mainwaring style leader Capt. Ron Smith they spent the day amusing the lieges with pyrotechnic displays from the flashing blue lights, hooter, headlights and hazard warning lights. Had they just had the foresight to use the hose to spray water over it, The Big Red Thing - to use their own technical term for the Fire Engine - would have offered serious competition to Waltzing Waters and would undoubtedly have added immensely to the entertainment value of the day. Sad to say that the excesses of power used to mount this interesting spectacle flattened the battery thus rendering the fire engine immobile. Captain Smith, showing his usual acumen, organised a "Charity Push" charging local heavyweights £1 each to try to push the fire engine one hundred yards while Willie McPherson discreetly tried to bump start it. At this point the bewhiskered Captain, demonstrating the leadership qualities, which have become a byword in fire fighting circles, evaporated into the crowd with the bitter departing instruction, "Get that bloody thing started."

****

After AMR's recent rock concert some local criticism was voiced suggesting that this did not bring the type of people which Aviemore wanted. A story comes of two young lads asking in a local sports shop for some cheap tents in order to have somewhere to sleep on the great night. The shop apologised pointing out that the cheapest models were £200. "OK we'll take two," said the braw lads. Either the price of hotel accommodation is getting higher than I had realised or perhaps this is exactly the type of free-spending people that Aviemore needs even if it doesn't want them.

****

The increasing number of dry stone dykes appearing all round Aviemore have greatly improved the appearance of the place but suspicions have been raised regarding where the District's Leisure & Recreation Chief Bozo Ron Stuart is finding all these new walls. Worried residents have noted that along the new Grantown by-pass at Craggan, dry-stone dykes have been disappearing at roughly the same rate as they have been growing in Aviemore, and are being replaced with wire and post barriers. Questions must be asked. Are Grantown dykes being used to provide Aviemore with ethnic walls? Is Ron Stuart a 'fence' for stolen dykes? Does anybody read this rubbish?

****

With the recent celebrity sightings in Strathspey of Sean Connery and Nigel Mansell as reported in last week's Strathie, it is hardly surprising that a number of other speculative and highly imaginative sightings have been reported. At the recent Rothiemurchus Highland Games a breathless visitor approached Aviemore's self-styled Provost, Ian Malcolm, exclaiming with some delight, that she had seen a celebrity in the crowd. She was certain that there in front of her was world class golfer Craig Stadler. The Provost, who still awaits his ceremonial gold chain from a grateful electorate, sadly shook his head. The visitor protested. "It must be," she said, "He's short, fat and has a walrus moustache." At the risk of seeming heightist, weightist and moustacheist, I have to report the reply. "No," said the disgruntled provost, "It's no' Craig Stadler, it's Ken Smith from the Strathie wearing a straw hat and sunglasses to give him an air of mystery."

****

The marble lined entrance hall of Strathie Tower lies immediately next door to Grantown's optician and although the opulence of our offices is a byword, a certain similarity between the two establishments can be detected. Enough to show that the desperate need for improved eyesight amongst Grantonians is a matter of urgency as a steady procession of the optically challenged are to be found sitting patiently in our comfy chairs awaiting their appointment. This has become such a regular feature of life at Strathie Tower that Debbie, our gorgeous, kindly receptionist, takes them gently by the hand out into the High Street and delivers them next door. Most never realise that they have been in the wrong place but many comment that the corridor is very draughty.

****

60

The Political Correctness Officer at Strathie Tower (she, he or it has an office near the boiler in the second basement level) has reprimanded me for the above article. Apparently, some sections of the community are now objecting to the use of the word person with its obvious derivation from the masculine 'son' and are now insisting that we use the term perkin. Now we will be unable to tell if we are dealing with people or biscuits. Readers are asked for any suggestions that they might offer to improve the language and cut out any of these obviously sexist (or is it personist, or indeed is it perkinist) words. Will we ever see Wilkinkin's Sword razor blades or will Autumn and Winter become seakins? Who will read a Shakespeare kinnet? On the other hand will I have to kinter along the road where I used to dotter?

****

The continuing hot weather is bringing out some incredible sights on local streets and public places. People of both sexes (I have to be careful. The Political Correctness Officer is looking over my shoulder) are baring all, or at least as much as anyone can be expected to take, in the interest of coolness and suntanning. Some of these people, or perkins, should know better and I am reminded of the words of my friend, the Lt. Commander.
"The memsahib was lying there like a beached whale," he said.
"Jimmy," I rebuked, "That's a bit cruel." After a pensive moment he replied.
"Cruel .... but fair."

And more water disaster this time in Frank Clark's Whisky Centre at Inverdruie, where drouthy connoisseurs gather from time to time to check the quality of Scotland's most important and entertaining export. A stalwart of Frank's organisation is the aesthetically challenged Captain Ron Smith of the Aviemore Fire Brigade and a man whose exploits have been noted in this column in the past. Sad to report, a deluge caused by a burst pipe was discovered on the premises one morning last week. Luckily it was only water which flooded through the sumptuous tasting rooms and not the amber liquid. At around the midday hour, shortly after the good Captain's withdrawal to enjoy a glass of lunch, neighbour Dudley Evans, who had been among the first to discover the problem, popped his head in the door to give encouragement and advice. "Where's the sponge?" he asked. Frank replied impassively. "He's gone to lunch."

****

Last week's article on the development of ski-ing in Speyside by one of the sport's pioneers, Frith Finlayson, caused some excitement among the diminutive souls who inhabit the 7th floor of Strathie Tower when he referred to his arrival in Aviemore station and "the wee sma' hoors." What the think tank are anxious to discover is:

(a) Who were these wee sma' hoors? and

(b) Are they still working?

****

62

They say that you can tell a man by the company he keeps but when we consider Grantown's best known old sea dog and member of the Strathspey literati Bill Mitchell, perhaps it should be, "You can tell a man who boozes by the company he chooses" In Captain Billy's case, the company he chooses includes such luminaries of the world of potability as our invalid editor Ken Smith and drouthie local leisure guru Ron Stuart. In this sort of company we are tempted to quote an old naval signal to him: "You are standing into danger." Then there's that other old naval saying, "Yo ho ho and a bottle of rum, beware the perils of drink old chum." Cap'n Billy, readers will instantly recall, set us the puzzle for this year's Christmas Limerick Competition with a choice of local topicality or bizarre spelling. The resounding success of this year's competition can only be properly measured by the number of entries. Two! Both competitors did however offer us a considerable choice of verse. In the light of this our panel of judges (me) decided that both should have one of their great works printed. Our first is by **Christine MacKenzie** of Aviemore, a one time thespian with the Aviemore Players. She has entered two pieces, one topical and one with bizarre spelling and it is the latter which we print below:

There was an old man - Ben Macdhui,
Whose antics were frightfully Schrui,
His wild mountain thymes,
Made no reason or rhymes,
So he landed head first in the Druie.

63

The second competitor is **Len Grassick**, the man who keeps them all right at Grantown Grammar. Len obviously has an easy job as he found the time to write ten different offerings. From this plethora of verse we picked the best and here it is:

An award for a flushing loo,
Sounds strange to me and you,
You just yank the chain,
To flush out the drain,
And the water pours over your shoe.

And now approaching Christmas, because we only got two entries, all of us here on the 10th floor feel hurt, unloved, unwanted, taken for granted, overworked, tired, ignored and depressed. In short, just like the average Speyside Mummy.

1996

The last time I mentioned Farquie MacBain of the Suie Hotel, I upset him. Not for any insult because, working behind a bar, you get used to that sort of thing. No! My solecism was misspelling his name. Not MacBean but MacBain. As I hope he will note, this time it is right. Moving away from spelling however rivetting the subject might be, a mole tells me of Farquie's recent holiday in the Canaries. Farquie was sunning himself on the island of Gomera in the company of JSMTC bus driver Charlie Robertson and during one of his exercise periods, inadvertently and (he tells us) soberly fell off a pavement and broke his foot in two places. Once order had been restored Farquie was obliged to hobble around in a 'stookie.' Readers who have had a leg in plaster will realise that it is almost impossible to have a bath or shower with this type of appendage and so before long, lack of washing can become a vexing issue even to those whose sensibilities have been dulled by years of living in Kincraig. After carefully weighing up all the possibilities, Farquie asked Charlie, "Next time you are out, get me a sponge." At the conclusion of Charlie's next jaunt to view the outside world, he returned with a small paper bag and the immortal words: "I couldn't find a sponge so I got you some teacakes." Those of you who have heard Farquie in critical mode will have no difficulty in filling in some apposite phrases at this point.

POETRY CORNER After my complaints in the last issue about the lack of entries for the limerick competition, I have been completely overwhelmed by verse. One entry for the competition which the 10th floor somehow managed to lose has reappeared. It follows the convention of bizarre spelling and is certainly worth printing although the competition is past. The offering from Jean Cormack of the Lodge Hotel, Newtonmore has therefore been decreed to be a New Year limerick:

> Hillwalkers high up on Creag Dhubh
> Are turning the air a bright blubh
>   Their paths crossed and fenced,
>   With barbed wire - They're incensed,
> And creating a hullaballubh.

And more. Judge and Mrs Robert Armstrong who live sometimes in Aviemore and sometimes in California, were so touched by my pathetic whinge in the last edition that they swiftly responded with some rhyming lines:

66

The Foolscap editor is glum,
For want of a limericking chum, (I think I can see where this is going)
    High in the tower
    Scribbling by the hour
Spending too much time on his bum. (I was right)

In a spirit as sweet as honey,
Here's a limerick that costs you no money,
    But even with practice,
    The very sad fact is,
The clean ones are not very funny.

****

We know that the subject of Scottish Poverty is one which is bending the great minds of economists all over the country but are things worse than we thought. As many readers will know, Carr-Bridge hosts a Porridge Making contest each year which it is pleased to call a World Championship and this will be its third year. Andrew Kirk, as a hard working member of the Tourist Association, was busily engaged in sending out press releases cheerfully announcing **Carr-Bridge's Third World Porridge Making Championships.** Carr-Bridge suffers from considerable social deprivation as we know but up until now we hadn't realised that it had become a 'Third World' village. All those wealthy readers out there who wish to send food parcels or adopt a child should contact the Carr-Bridge Community Council for more information. Who knows. If things get much worse, they may have to drop the hyphen. But never fear, help is at hand. A few miles down the road, that sophisticated, civilised village, Aviemore is believed to be sending a team of emergency missionaries North as we write.

****

Aviemorons will be feeling some sympathy for the islanders on Eigg. Last week's news that some of the island's estate workers had not been paid brought into question the solvency of the estate's new owner, the German artist Martin Eckhart Maruma. Students of the Scottish socio-political scene will recall that the last owner Keith Schellenberg was equally flamboyant and possible just as financially fascinating. Eigg has suffered at the hands of various owners whose interests did not necessarily coincide with those of the residents. Grandiose plans have been announced by all the owners but time passes and nothing happens. The whole place goes on deteriorating thus lowering the prospects of employment and social advancement of the people who, live and work there and who seem to be powerless in the face of the outside interests. Now! What does that remind me of?

****

As a concerned member of the local populace, I found myself at the recording of **Ruth Wishart's Speaking Out** programme for Radio Scotland which many of you may have listened to on Monday morning. The great debate concerned the Cairngorm funicular railway planning application and the huge turnout showed the importance which the community attaches to this project. Whilst I, in common with most residents of the area, am a conservationist, I also want to earn a living and see skiing develop and do not believe that the two are mutually incompatible. The extreme conservation lobby got a bit of a drubbing but we here on the 10th floor feel that the fault lies with the government. Years ago when I was young it happened occasionally that a distressed person would stand on a street corner and harangue the passing hordes with predictions of doom and exhortations to lead their lives according to the speaker's principles. Other quieter souls would march around glumly bearing placards warning that the end of the world was nigh. In these far off times a couple of kindly souls in white coats would usually arrive and escort these prophets of doom to a secure place where they could be cared for. Since the government started their Care in the Community programme, which we here wholeheartedly support, thousands have benefited by being able to mix in what passes for normal society but I am sure that it was never the government's intention that these poor misguided souls should band themselves together in groups and try to tell the rest of us how we should live.

****

69

_____

The good burghers of Aviemore are beginning to suspect that their 'Provost' Ian Malcolm is planning a new career as a Baywatch Himbo. This can be the only explanation for sightings of his hirsute form ploughing up and down the swimming pool in the Four Seasons Hotel most mornings and evenings. Other less kindly voters who have witnessed this awesome spectacle, have suggested that a more believable explanation might be that he is auditioning for the title role in the remake of, "It Came From 20,000 Fathoms." All these impressions are however quite wrong. Our worthy tribune is starting a new venture as a financial wizard under the name of Malcolm-Delporte Associates, a title which suggests to our innocent eyes an international flavour to the business. As if this was not enough, he is also becoming a star of Radio on Speysound FM where he can be heard on Hendy Pollock's Friday evening show at 7.00pm passing ribald comment on the week's news. As most readers will know Speysound stars are unpaid so we hope that his new business enterprise will prove to be more profitable than his career on radio.

A certain employee of Cairngorm Chairlift who has appeared in this column before is gaining a reputation for gullibility. Apart from paying nearly £300 for a pair of reading glasses he has further confounded his admirers while trying to make his thinning hair grow. The matter came to light when his wife noticed a hint of the Asha Restaurant around the bedclothes. Closer inspection revealed that it was coming directly from her spouse's head and all the surrounding bed linen. He explained patiently to her increasingly angry back that he had been told that curry powder was a certain cure for baldness. Before other readers jeopardise their marriages, we feel that it is only fair to point out that, try as we might, no scientific evidence has been uncovered to support this theory.

****

Our many eagle eyed readers will have noticed that their favourite organ (well- maybe second favourite) The Strathie increased its cover price two weeks ago, rising by a dramatic two pence to 34p. The more observant may have noticed that last week, by an oversight, the price hadn't been changed on the mast head and bargains were had by readers buying Strathies at the old price. Sadly for us here on the 10th floor this has meant a loss of tuppence for every copy sold and may well have cost the company in excess of £3.68. Soon I expect Ken Smith to demand that I turn down the temperature in my en-suite jacuzzi in order to save money. I must fight this encroachment on my civil liberties. It is down to 72 degrees already.

This column was invited along to Coylumbridge recently to attend a 'This is your Life' surprise party for Eilif Moen who has been Ski School Director of the Scottish Norwegian Ski School for many years. The evening was organised by Aviemore's Sloanie, Fiona Coats and was attended by the great and the good, the doyens of the ski trade and valley oldsters. We are not prepared to divulge under which, if any, of these headings your favourite column was invited however suffice it to say that the evening was a great success and that Eilif maintained his gentlemanly calm throughout. Frith Finlayson made a speech encompassing the history of skiing locally. In the midst of the story he said, "There was a lot of trouble in the ski trade around here at that time." After a moment's serious thought he added with refreshing candour, "I was the cause of most of it, right enough."

****

Readers are warned that an outbreak of MBSE, or Mad LEC disease as it is known, has been reported in the area. The first symptom is the sudden appearance of a royal and green anorak (sometimes called anoraksia nervosa) and having the words Moray Badenoch & Strathspey Enterprise embroidered on it. Soon the victim starts to use strange words which neither it nor the listener clearly understands such as: outcomes, evaluate, underpinning knowledge, etc. Before long entire sentences become virtually unintelligible. Towards the end, the victim spews out acres of useless paper which invariably threatens to choke those around it. Members of the public are warned to stay away from any sufferer

72

as contact with MBSE is certain to involve the onset of Ruane (pronounced ruin).

****

John Robertson, author of the shinty history, "Kingussie and the Caman" is also said to be an aspiring novelist. He recently had some inspiration for a mystery story in the style of "Kidnapped." John popped out the other night to purchase some comestibles from nearby Murchie's grocery shop intending to return within approximately two minutes. In the street he was hailed by the Chieftain of Kingussie Shinty club, Joey Taylor, in his car. Joey called "Jump in," and John obliged happily. Joey drove off but didn't stop till he got to Fort William where a meeting of the Shinty Year Book Committee was in progress, a meeting which John had gone to some trouble to avoid. Between the meeting and a few drams here and there John eventually got home from his two minute jaunt at 3.30 in the morning.

****

Farquie MacBain has broken his leg again. Avid readers may recall that I reported Farquie's previous limb fracture while he was on holiday last year. That report had him hopping mad as I had inadvertently described him as a descendant of Bean rather than Bain. The sad news is that the licensee of the Suie Hotel in Kincraig has once again broken his leg, this time while walking across his garden or so he claims. We do not know what his condition was at the time but we can safely say that he is plastered once more. Unkind critics of this blatt's style of journalism have suggested that the Strathie headline for the story should read, "Barman's broken leg hits pub".

****

April Fool's day passed without any particular incident being reported to us here on the 10th floor, so we are reduced to recalling tales from last year. It will come as no surprise to regular readers to discover that it concerns playful electrician Finlay Binnie. Last March 31st, Finlay was working at the home of Jim Coyle who owns the Balavil Hotel. In his usual humorous manner, Finlay wired up a klaxon horn to a timer and hid it under Jim and Helen's bed, timing the device to go off at the ungodly hour of 4 am on the 1st. The Coyles have a repeater of the hotel fire alarm in their garage and so when the klaxon sounded at dark o'clock in the morning, Jim scrambled to his feet and stumbled round trying to engage his legs in trousers, fearing the worst. As he crashed around the bedroom in the dark, Helen stayed calm. "The noise," she opined, "is not outside this bedroom." Considering the matter in the cold light of reason, Jim was forced to agree and didn't take too long in locating the offending hooter. Finlay's machiavellian mind was still one step ahead. The klaxon was in a box with plumber Alan Smith's name on the side. Although Alan had also been working in the house the previous day and although Jim was half awake and in a blind panic, the ploy was not entirely successful. The first words that Jim uttered were, "That B*****d Binnie!"

74

Any reader confiding stories of this year's madness to us, can be assured that it will go no further than this column.

* * * * * * * * * * * * * * * * *

Strathspey Thistle's monthly draw is a great attraction to some of our inveterate gamblers. This was especially the case recently because the jackpot had rolled over, lottery style, accumulating to an impressive £700. Zealous readers of this blatt may have noticed the photo last week of the two happy winners sharing their good fortune. Not far away our recently retired leisure guru Ron Stuart was gnashing his teeth with a bit of weeping and wailing on the side. There could have been three winners as Ron had also picked the same five winning numbers. Sadly for Ron, using his widely renowned facility with figures and numbers and possibly affected by his enthusiasm for the gamble he had added a sixth to his selection and was thus disqualified. The two winners were so sorry for him that they could hardly stop laughing as they cashed their cheques.

Motorists passing Kingussie last week may have been confused by the sight of a swimmer in the Glebe pond. Some local passers by thought that it might be an attempt to 'nobble' the ducks before the grand occasion of the duck race. Others wondered if this was a sighting of one of Kingussie's famous tourist class mermaids on another visit home. Whatever was happening, it required the investigation by duck race supremo Sandy Bennet, who in his alter ego - Kingussie's traffic warden - became momentarily famous when he booked the actor Sean Connery for parking in the High Street last year. Sandy discovered to his horror that the culprit seen floundering in the pond was none other than his dear wife Isobel who claimed that she had been feeding the ducks, overstretched and had inadvertently fallen headlong into the water where she considered the best method of getting out was to swim to the other side. Sandy, it seems was satisfied with this explanation, but there are still some unanswered questions such as: exactly what do you feed to plastic ducks? Or alternatively, do Kingussie have real ducks in their duck race?

****

Molly Ducket of Grantown still reels from the shock of seeing two beat policeman on the town's streets on Tuesday night. This traditional old world scene would have been confusing enough if the two constables concerned hadn't stopped her and enquired if she had by any chance seen a cow. Fearing an outbreak of mad cop disease, Molly dashed to the police station to check the sobriety of her inquisitors only to discover that the mystery of the missing

76

cow was indeed extant. The beast sauntered out through an open gate at Tuesday's market and since then has been spotted only once near the Craiglynne Hotel. Apart from this one sighting the cow evades capture even as we go to press. It is obviously holed up somewhere or has fallen in with a bad lot as no incidence of an animal sidling up to police and saying, "It's a fair cop guv and no mistake," or "put the cuffs on copper, I'll come quietly," have yet been reported. The public are warned that harbouring a known cow is a punishable offence. We have to accept that as far as the cow is concerned; no moos is good moos.

****

John Robertson, Kingussie's man of letters, is obviously not a techno freak. He recently bought himself a new electric kettle. As soon as he got home from making this exciting purchase he found himself in need of a cup of tea so unpacked the new utensil only to be disappointed. There was no lead, no cable no plug, just a kettle. John popped out to the electrical shop and bought a suitable cable. Once home, he filled the kettle through its spout as he always does and made his refreshing brew. A tidy person, it was two weeks later when he got around to throwing out the box and while examining the outside of the box discovered that the device should have come complete with a lead. He removed all the packing and tore the box in shreds searching for it but all to no avail. Sitting there sipping his cup of tea, a horrible suspicion began to dawn. With a wild surmise, he lifted the lid and there inside, neatly coiled and now virtually melted was the cable for his kettle. As far as we are able to divine, he lost enthusiasm for his cup of tea at that point.

****

A story of Euro 96 comes to us a little late but none the worse for that. One Grantown football fan is a Rangers supporter and Gazza fan so it was with mixed emotions that he entered into a private wager with a friend, that Gazza would score against Scotland when we played England. Sitting in the crowded pub on the day of the Scotland v. England match the atmosphere grew sombre as the game continued. When Gazza scored, the jubilant gambler shouted **"YES"** at the top of his voice. It was immediately followed by a chilling silence. According to the story, our gambler wisely decided not to wait to explain the reasons surrounding his outburst and legged it to another establishment as fast as possible.

****

Needle matches are not unknown in other sports and whilst we would hesitate to suggest that shinty supporters occasionally succumb to these baser feelings, it can be considered that a degree of rivalry exists between Kingussie and Newtonmore. Matters have not been helped last week during the Clan MacPherson all singing, all dancing, centenary gathering. The organisers who are obviously from out of town chose to erect a triple marquee in Ardvonie Park, Kingussie which was blue and white striped. For the uninitiated, blue and white are the colours of Newtonmore whilst red and blue is worn by Kingussie. By a spooky coincidence, it is being rumoured that the marquee at the Newtonmore Highland Games last week was coloured red and white. Shinty supporters are said to be in a highly confused state. Much as they are on a Saturday afternoon.

****

Travellers south may have noticed that the major piece of dual carriageway on the A9, between Dalnaspidal and Dalnacardoch - where we can normally pass all the caravans, lorries and crawling cars thus relieving the frustration that causes accidents - is under repair and that one complete carriageway is closed for the three weeks beginning the 22nd of July. While appreciating that road works must be done we wonder just which Scottish Office official was responsible for this piece of inspired scheduling. With 52 weeks in the year to choose from they have, with unerring accuracy, pounced on the three busiest weeks of the season to close Scotland's main arterial tourist route. We should be able to identify the culprit soon. In the civil service, genius of this magnitude is usually rewarded in the New Year's honours list.

****

It is not readily known that Provost Malcolm of Aviemore has for some years enjoyed the benefits of mayoral transport, to wit a second hand mountain bike. Due to a slight predilection for certain brands of beer, the Provost sometimes tours his constituency of an evening checking that Aviemore's rigorous licensing laws are being properly observed and can frequently be seen weaving his homeward way on this particular transport of delight. Last week things went agley - as our bard might have put it - when the gold chain around his neck got entangled with the oily version around the pedals and the bike was forcibly abandoned at the rear of the Cairngorm Hotel where it remained for several days while the provost had his ermine trimmed robe dry cleaned. When Ian, as we in the newspaper trade are allowed to call him, felt well enough to bring the bike home he checked its position behind the hotel but was then persuaded to discuss politics with a few of the electorate who had gathered for that purpose in the bar. Later when he was in a suitable enough condition to ride the thing he went to the rear of the premises only to discover that it had gone. The Cairngorm's kindly owner, Peter Steinle was quick to inform the police about this dastardly theft and they in turn were brisk in arriving to investigate. Peter in an attempt to 'help the police with their enquiries' drove around the environs and was soon back with the contraption which he had discovered at the rear of the Four Seasons Hotel. Officers are said to be confused and suspicious (no changes there then) and are wondering if this was a Steinle prank or if indeed Provost Malcolm had simply left his bike behind the wrong pub.

****

Now back to Carr-Bridge where the annual Festival of Music is rearing its ugly head once more, indeed it begins this very weekend.

This column has an advance copy of the programme. On the front page, a small and almost unreadable logo (for someone with poor eyesight such as this column) says "Sex Matters" and who are we to disagree. The eyesight in question may well have been damaged - if old wives tales are to be believed - by too much of this very thing. A full page inside the front cover goes into greater detail offering advice?, free condoms, and a subject called emergency contraception which we don't entirely understand but may well be something like an all-night pizza delivery service. Other subjects mentioned are pregnancy and sexually transmitted diseases. All in all, the advertisement definitely suggests that the Carr-Bridge Festival of Music is an occasion when lust is unbridled and joy is unconfined. If it is indeed a time for pleasure seekers and hedonists rivalled only by the Rio carnival, then, haud me back.

****

The Strathie's advertising executive Jacqui O'Rourke has just given birth to a 7lbs son. Those of our advertisers who have been pressured by Jacqui in a desperate attempt to meet her deadlines will not be surprised to learn that she produced the son and heir a few days early. While Jacqui has been otherwise engaged her place has been taken by a Kingussie lad, Craig Meeks whose golf has improved immeasurably during his time with this fearless organ of the press. It may be that the amount of work he has done has left him time to play on the course or it may be that he has been coached by the Strathie's own maestro of the links (he's a dab hand with the sausages), Ken Smith. Craig's ability to find the pin is overshadowed by his other geographical shortcomings. On a recent visit to darkest Nethybridge he could not find his customer and eventually got so lost that he couldn't find his way out of the village. He is reputed to have bought a map in order to find his way home and we anxiously await a look at this complex document. A Street Plan of Nethybridge.

STREET PLAN OF
NETHYBRIDGE.

****

The lads of Thistle were playing away last Wednesday in Lossiemouth. Team member, Iain Lambie of Speyside Heather Centre fame was badly injured in the course of the affray so one of the committee, in a moment of uncharacteristic altruism, offered to forego the remaining portion of the game and drive poor Iain to Dr. Gray's Hospital in Elgin. During the lengthy process of admission a nurse appeared notebook in hand and pencil poised. "I wonder if you could give me some details?" asked the nurse. The bold Iain replied, "Well when I left we were three- nil up."

****

Our ex local newshound Paul Hunter is off finding fame and fortune in Glasgow working on the magazine for the homeless, 'The Big

Issue.' During his sojourn in Aviemore, Paul was wont to plunge himself in the cold (OK lukewarm) waters of the Four Seasons swimming pool and so naturally in his first week in Scotland's premier city he was keen to continue this curious masochistic pleasure. The particular bathing establishment which Paul chose to patronise, operated the convention of wearing the locker key on an elastic band around the wrist. In all fairness to such establishments there is no rule which says the band must be worn on the wrist and no doubt some of our less genteel readers will already be allowing their imaginations to dwell on the prospect of wearing the thing around other bodily appendages however it must be said that Paul stuck with convention. Sadly, the band broke and Paul's key drifted to the bottom of the pool a fact of which he remained unaware till much later. Sadder still, the key must have been found by a thief because when the locker was eventually opened, Paul's trousers were gone. Strathclyde Police are said to be looking for a person with a diminished sense of responsibility and virtually no taste.

****

To rewrite an old saying, "When a shark kills a man it is called ferocity. When a man pulls a fish from the water and bangs its head on a stone, it is called sport." Nonetheless, local sportsmen have been as sick as parrots recently. After a long dry, if cold, summer the fishing season finally drew to a close with the last day of September. It has been a hard time for anglers. Rivers reduced to a trickle, burns dried up, almost no movement, hardly a fish to be seen. But what have we seen since the first day of October? Is it:

(a) Tons of b——y rain

(b) Funny sort of weather

(c) The Buckie fish van

Eagle eyed meteorologists should send their answers on a postcard to the secretary of the Strathspey Angling Club.

****

I read with interest in this blatt last week the announcement of the GlenMore Gondola, an apparently "better alternative," complete with glossy brochure. The previous week I read that the opponents of Cairngorm Chairlift's funicular railway development are taking their fight on to a world stage and will ask for it to be banned at a conference in Montreal. Amongst the many 'spoilsport' objections that these various bodies have produced is the rather contentious one: "does it represent good value for money in terms of public spending". Given that all these bodies are publicly funded - either by government grant or by donations from such as we, can we ask is their service value for money in similar terms. Are the various multi billion pound budgets which support these organisations doing those of us who cough up any good. How many highly paid officials will be travelling to Montreal on expenses (our expense) to vote against a commercial activity which will only bring jobs, sport and fun. Yes maybe it's the idea of someone else having fun that they don't like. Or is it that the public will be able to walk in their private fiefdoms. How much will it cost for these minor functionaries and pompous clerks to have their transatlantic jaunt and the chance to produce vast quantities of self righteous hyperbole. And the glossy brochure - well, not too glossy of course as it is printed on recycled paper - but still must have cost us a pretty penny. Who exactly benefits from these exercises in the luxury of taking the morale high ground. I for one can say without fear of contradiction that the Montreal trip and the brochure are both an obvious waste of money. They could have saved the lot. If they just keep quiet, do nothing and say nothing, the Chairlift management - to those of us watching from the sidelines - seem quite capable of running the whole thing into the ground without any outside help.

****

This is more like it. Last week's Strathie had the kind of letters page which makes a newspaper desirable. Invective flowing in all directions and on a number of unrelated matters. If we could keep up this level of angst in print, there would be no need for Foolscap. (You're fired, - Ed.) Everything from estate management to foxes, not forgetting the odd passing swipe at the two long running soap operas, AMR and the Cairngorm funicular without which no issue of this blatt would be complete. Keep up the tirade folks. It's stuff like this that made the Strathie what it is today. (A useful firelighter) I must say, returning briefly to the brochure for the GlenMore Gondola, I did rather like the star system used for scoring it against the Funicular. Things like Environmental benefits; Funicular 1, Gondola 5. In every category the Gondola beats the

Funicular hands down, the total number of points being 7 for the Funicular and an impressive 16 for the Gondola. Whitewash or what? There was just one small problem though. Who exactly designed the arbitrary star system and who awarded the points. Well, er um... the Gondola promoters actually. Obviously a totally objective judgement then.

****

A local lady golfer of no mean ability, Frances Hay, recently won a competition with husband Gordon but sporting success may not be without its drawbacks. It seems, perhaps due to concentrating too hard on golf, that Frances is losing her memory. She forgot her sister's birthday last week. Nothing unusual about that I hear you say. Many of us often forget family birthdays, in fact it almost counts as normal behaviour. I would agree except that in this case there are extenuating circumstances. Frances and her sister are twins.

****

From time to time during the darker days of the Aviemore Centre, the 10th floor decided that the column really needed an agony aunt to sort out the depression that was rampant in the valley. With this in mind Aunty Foolscap was born and a number of disturbed people wrote in describing their concerns, often in unnecessary detail.

Dear Aunty Foolscap

I am a young attractive girl who cannot seem to meet any nice boys in this area. I am very affectionate and passionate but can never find a partner who fully appreciates me. What should I do? Worried, Grantown.

Aunty Foolscap replies:

Dear Worried, Grantown,

This is a very serious case and so I think that the only answer is for you to come up to the 11th floor of Strathie Tower so that we can discuss this more fully in my en-suite jacuzzi.

****

Struan House in Carr-Bridge seems to be the place for sport. Once more we find some entertainment from this bijou hostelry. Graham Davidson the mine host and his daughter Helen, who works for another well known newspaper rivalling only this fearless organ of the press, were out and about testing Helen's new company car. (Where's my Strathy car? - Flscp.) In Inverness, they parked in the Safeway car park and decided to test the leg room and comfort in the back seats. Once every possible criterion had been satisfied they moved to exit only to discover that they were locked inside by the child-proof locks.

When the creator was fashioning the Davidson family, he did not stint himself. He was, to say the least, lavish in his apportioning and constructed them on fairly generous lines. This meant that scrambling over the headrests into the front was not an option. No doubt some of our lateral thinking readers are ahead of us here. What on earth could they do trapped in the rear of a child proofed car in Safeway Car Park? Simple. They wound down the window and opened the door from outside .... but don't tell the kids.

****

According to the front page of this august journal, (What! The Strathie? - Ed.) the new Aviemore Centre will cost £24 million and will create 100 jobs all of which will be filled by local people. This represents almost a quarter of a million pounds per job and since one might assume an 'average' wage of £200 per week represents 24 years work to repay the money before any particular benefit can accrue. I have a much better idea. Far better to pick 100 local people at random and give each £240,000 and see what happens. Some will start businesses that will give employment, some will drink it away in a short time boosting the profits of local hoteliers and assorted retailers. Others, well .... I for one am willing to volunteer for this particular social experiment and will happily continue to write this column from some distant, exotic location to keep those less fortunate up to date with my new hedonistic life style.

****

The assertion from AMR chief Executive Don Lawson, that **ALL** the new staff will be hired from the local area introduces another new concept. That of hiring on the basis of address rather than ability. It is an interesting idea and has its obvious advantages, not the least being that it will bring the job of personnel selection well within Don's skills. "Hello, come in, sit down. What's your address? Aviemore? Well, er um... you've got the job then."

****

Interestingly, the feast of Saint Nicholas (Yawn - Ed.) is really on the 5th of December and as our more erudite readers will immediately realise, old Saint Nick was the pre-production model of Santa Claus. He is of course the patron saint of children which is why he sneaks into people's houses at night leaving toys lying around just where you'll trip over them and break your neck. (So he's the one who does that? - Ed.) The truly intellectual will know that he is the patron saint of Russia but few perhaps will realise that he is also the patron saint of unmarried mothers and sailors. This is an interesting discovery. The think tank consider that there could well be a connection between these two last groups. On the subject of just what that connection might be, the think tank have so far remained silent so we can only guess however if we have got the right idea I suppose the connection with children applies too. But where do the Russians fit in?

1997

Two apposite remarks overheard at a local Christmas dinner. "Do you take water in your whisky?" "Only if there's room." And: "The trouble with New Year's resolutions is that wives have a habit of remembering them."

****

The announcement that Michael Forsyth has 'ring fenced' £8m for Aviemore is excellent news. Surely now, after all these years, the community can afford lamp-posts, a gold chain and some flashy robes for Provost Malcolm who has been anxiously awaiting this sort of recognition for many years now.

****

Colonel Ian Strain, who in his younger days was known as the opticians friend, Major I. Strain, will be known to many local bon viveurs as a cheery companion. Ian lives in Boat of Garten since retiring from the army and recently had a strong urge to get back to his roots and eat an old fashioned plate of mince and tatties. He strolled into the Tesco supermarket in Aviemore but was dismayed to find that of mince there was none. Being a Colonel, he quite naturally called for the Manageress and complained that such a traditional and desirable staple food was missing. It was explained that it was all the fault of the computer ordering system however bearing the complaint in mind somebody must have re-booted the computer because lo and behold last week when the good Colonel arrived to do his shopping he found mince as far as the eye could see and because of the mince mountain the price had, quite naturally, collapsed. Mince was selling for a derisory amount. Feeling slightly guilty in case his complaint was responsible for the glut, Ian bought 40lbs of the stuff although it is fair to say that the bargain price might also have influenced his decision. After watching him struggle home with half a cow reduced to its component parts, let's hope that the mince king of Kinchurdy Road, as he is now known, doesn't discover that he has lost his taste for this world renowned Scottish delicacy or residents at his guest house may find ground beef products featuring quite strongly on the breakfast menu.

****

La Thuile, Italy
Old Men Behaving Badly
I am disporting myself here on the snow covered pistes. These runs are almost empty and the sun shines from morning 'til night. I am ski-ing in the company of two other local worthies who cannot be named for legal reasons. Naturally they are both more badly behaved than I. La Thuile is on the border with France and

therefore we occasionally ski over to La Rosiere, the resort on the French side, in order to have lunch and admire the view. The view takes in Les Arcs opposite us and we can see some of the peaks of Val Thorens. Turning our relaxed gaze to the left we casually identify the valley running up towards Tignes and Val D'Isere before sipping our glasses of wine. Back over in La Thuile we ski in the shadow of Mont Blanc but can clearly see the Matterhorn in the distance. This resort is an alpine geography lesson and it has the advantage of motorway style pistes almost devoid of skiers. One day going up on the chair with one of my couthy companions I espy a snowboarder doing a head plant in the unpisted area below us and politely remark, "Look at the boarder." My cultured companion points to the top of the hill and the route to La Rosiere. "Na na laddie," He insists, "The border's away ower yonder."

****

Education is a wonderful thing and therefore should be available even to teachers. One chemistry teacher who, for the purposes of saving his embarrassment, we will not name has just had his education improved. The said gentleman had trouble starting his car and so was prompted to call on Calum Campbell, the hooker for Strathspey Rugby team. Calum brought his car and his jump leads into play fixing one lot of clips to his own battery terminals and offering the teacher the opposite ends. When the car still wouldn't start, Calum inspected the leads to discover that the chemistry teacher was a bit shaky on the principles of conductivity.

He had attached the leads to the plastic casing of his battery. Calum obligingly pointed out that they would work better if they were fixed to the metal terminals. They got the car started.

****

Talking of this dear hyphenated town, a reader (what another reader? - Ed.) has complained about Alan Boxx on his Sunday morning Speysound FM radio show anglicising the name to Grantown upon Spey. Apparently we don't have upons in Scotland, only ons. Be warned Boxxy. Your listener may desert you and then where will you be? Or maybe it is a deliberate policy on the part of Grantonians who recently introduced the hyphens in an effort to keep up with our other double barrelled village, Carr-Bridge, and are now going that one step forward. Where will it all end I ask you? Newt-on-the-more? Dal-over-whinnie? Crom-in-the-dale? Boat unter den Garten? Jawohl! Other suggestions on a postcard please to: Boxxy c/o Speysound FM, Aviemore

****

I have told before of the impressive distribution of this mighty organ of the press. Some people scorn our circulation without realising that the Strathie travels to the ends of the earth. For the past six weeks it has been winging its way to Cyprus where kenspeckle figure and ex Regional councillor Sandy Lindsay, has been resting his old bones. Six weeks is too long for Sandy to be

93

parted from our high quality journalism (yes yes, you've done this already, - Ed.) and so he arranged to have a copy delivered so that he could read it while reclining by the pool in a hammock slung between two spice girls. One day Sandy's circle of friends felt a tremor but their fears were allayed by a young sun tanned beauty who said, "Don't worry it's probably just an earthquake." Sandy claims that he could hardly be concerned at his age if a youngster treated the threat with such disdain. The think tank have another theory. They have suggested that one of the bikini clad girls made the earth move for Sandy and he is trying to keep it quiet.

****

Workers at Grantown sewage works were distracted from their work recently. This is not an easy thing to do to those whose lives are dedicated to sewage but nonetheless it happened. The cause for the excitement was the sight of a well known local fencing contractor leaping and jumping about as though in pain while constructing the new fence around the aforementioned works. The squad puzzled over this strange phenomenon for some moments but were unable to divine the cause. It was too early for wasp stings. There was no sign of a hammer or its natural concomitant the throbbing thumb. There was no good reason for the behaviour and having spent quite enough time wrestling with this thorny problem our lads returned to their toil as is their wont. Later that day, still bristling with curiosity, they approached the contractors companions to discover the cause of the energetic display. The boys cheerfully explained their boss's enigmatic behaviour. The man had recently taken up line dancing and was passing on some steps to his workmates.

I had promised to myself that during the run up to the E****ion I would make every effort not to mention politics. This is partly because, for the last few weeks, our letters page has become clogged with acres and acres of useless verbiage which no-one in their right mind would consider reading. The only folk who do read this rubbish are the party activists who are unlikely to change their views so it serves no purpose whatsoever. It is also partly because I have no interest in politics. As every other newspaper covers the various childish political posturings of those who would govern us I felt that this column should be a haven for all sensible and reasonable people and that not a word of these events should sully this page. However being short of copy this week, I have abandoned my principles in favour of giving you even more acres of useless verbiage. (Nothing new there then. - Ed.)

A group of SNP types, their car plastered with SNP posters, passed through Carr-Bridge on Sunday all dressed in tattered kilts and torn shirts. They had all the appearance of extras from 'Braveheart' on an outing to Blackpool, and were buying packets of fags like true 13th century Scots. Naturally with such nationalistic fervour being portrayed, the SNP is keen to identify with this successful film and all that it stands for. Things like: made by Americans written by an Australian and filmed predominantly in Ireland. And one other little feature. A complete disregard for actual events.

****

More politics. A Grantown school teacher was passing Black Park and noticed a huge poster with the name 'Mary Scanlon' writ large thereon. He claims he looked in the field but there was no Mary Scanlon to be seen. This is evidence that there may be the slightest stirrings of a sense of humour among the staff of Grantown's most popular Grammar School. Will it be enough to start a movement?

****

Fans of the Strathie crossword may have thought that last week's paper had a mistake just because we printed the answers but didn't print the crossword. Of course this was quite deliberate. As usual the Strathie is in the forefront of innovation and it is simply offering a new type of crossword. The competition works as follows. We give you all the answers and the first person who can make up a crossword from the clues wins a prize. So far it hasn't been a great success with absolutely no entries as yet so it looks as though we will have to revert to the original concept this week.

****

Still on things watery. That well known diva of the dance floor Lorna McKenna who doubles from her party girl image to being one of our local PE teachers, has been attempting a spot of synchronised drowning at Grantown Grammar School swimming pool. Her enthusiasm for jigging is matched by her enthusiasm for all things sporting and thus racing around the pool in haste to get her charges organised she managed to fall headlong and fully clothed into the pool. Although Lorna is a strong swimmer, it might have been a pleasant touch if at least one pupil had shown even the slightest inclination to leap in and save her.

****

Newtonmore, sin city of the North, was up to its usual party tricks when the Coyles at the Balavil Sport Hotel celebrated their Silver Wedding Anniversary. This major social event took the form of a fancy dress party with guests having to dress up as a character sharing their own initials. Thus it was that Jim Coyle went as Julius Caesar and our friendly local banker George West, true to his honest character, appeared as George Washington. Ruth Stewart turned up as a car - the RS2000 but had to be towed home. No doubt readers of the meanest intelligence are beginning to get the idea. Some of those invited didn't participate wholeheartedly. Alan Smith and Archie Stewart lacked enthusiasm for dressing up, claiming feebly that nobody had told them it was fancy dress however the general consensus of opinion was that they could therefore pass as Dumb and Dumber. Half way through the proceedings, the fire alarm sounded and the party decanted into the street in cheery form. This eruption of the population onto the highway nearly caused the death of the late President of the US when a speeding car missed him by inches and almost robbed the banking world of one of its most energetic characters. The near miss came as something of a disappointment to the Grim Reaper aka Gregor Rimmel who was out looking for suitable customers and might possibly have expected to wipe out his overdraft as a by-product. The whole sorry mess was started by boxer Evander Holyfield who, by getting steaming in the shower, had somehow set off the alarms. It is not known if he was accompanied by the essential accessories of the famous boxer, scantily clad bimbos, but he managed to create enough heat to sound the siren. We are holding another of our famous competitions to discover who knows the real identity of the slightly chewed boxer with the initials EH. Answers please on a postcard to Eddie Harrigan, Manager of the Balavil Sport Hotel.

****

A true story from the misty isle from whence I have recently returned.

Two ladies from a Skye based company went on an Assertiveness Training course. It was so successful that, some time after they returned, they decided to share the information with the rest of their staff and looked for the course notes to help them. This conversation followed.

"Where are the Assertiveness Training course notes?"

"I lent them to the nurse."

"That was weeks ago, why don't you ask for them back."

"I don't really like to."

****

When the news broke that pioneer astronaut Dr. John Glen is to take to space once more at the age of 70 there was some slight confusion at Aviemore Community Council. On hearing that a 70 year old Dr. Glen was going to be fired into space their hopes were cruelly raised that it might be their regional councillor Dr. Iain Glen who was about to boldly go and take a giant step for mankind. Further investigation however has disappointed the good burghers.

While strolling around Harrods I noticed a little something to interest fans of Aviemore's Lord Provost Ian Malcolm from the makers of Jurassic Park 2. They have produced an Ian Malcolm plastic doll which is available at all good toy stores so that the grateful voters of Aviemore can buy it and cherish it for years to come. Provost Malcolm will, no doubt, be willing to autograph copies of these for his more ardent followers.

****

It will not have escaped the attention of those readers who scan the pages of the Strathie for matters of great moment that the Aviemore Brewery recently started production of our very own locally brewed 'real ale'. The first pourings of the 'Ruthven' had been made too strong and was destined to be poured down the drain. Your correspondent was able to insert himself mid way in this process and managed to scoop a couple of pints of the stuff which turned out to be around 5.8% by vol. For those who do not understand such figures let me explain by saying that after two pints, the Foolscap marketing plan involved piping the beer into local houses like Cable TV or British Gas so that customers could drink direct from their own beer taps in the comfort of their own homes. Just what schemes we would have come up with had we had a third pint of this heady brew is hard to imagine. Brewery Chief Norman Swinton, is an inveterate entrepreneur. Some time ago he operated the 'Fryer Tuck' mobile fast food van at Sinclair's Corner which readers may recall came to a sudden demise. The brewery hopes to produce a lager soon which this column thinks should be called 'Friar Tuck' in memory of the previous business. The only danger will be that after a couple of pints it may be a tricky name to shout at the barman.

****

Kingussie's Buy a Brick Scheme to build a new community and sports centre has got off to a flying start undoubtedly due to the exceptional quality of their superb brochure. They are well on the way to their targets with over £10,000 promised within two weeks of the launch and are therefore thinking of increasing the target figure. The idea behind the scheme is that if you pay £50 you can have your name inscribed on a brick which will go into the entrance hall of the building and the cash raised from this will help to get the project off the ground. Some generous minded purchasers are paying more than the minimum £50 but others are less helpful. At least one person has either failed to grasp the concept of the scheme or is being deliberately provocative. Susan Paton was taking a very pro-active approach and going around the doors collecting. At one door a woman came out to her without either an envelope or a cheque but carrying a brown paper parcel. She handed the parcel to Susan saying, "This'll save me fifty quid," and disappeared back into her home firmly closing the door. Inside the parcel was a brick.

****

A not unreasonable complaint was heard in a Strathspey village recently from a bored teenager and here I quote verbatim. "The old folk complained that the young were hanging about in the streets. So what do they do? Build a £300,000 bowling green to keep the old people off the streets." It does seem that with most of society's problems perceived to be as a result of young people falling into bad habits, bad company and parents not knowing where their kids are at night, that our political masters might consider spending similarly vast sums on giving our young people the type of facilities that they want rather than those facilities that we think they should have.

****

Duncan Grant and Charlie Sinclair are two of Grantown's upstanding citizens who, between them, make up the powerhouse of the community council or to couch it in Aviemore terms, The Provost and Deputy Provost. For the last council meeting, the dynamic duo turned up at the Grammar School at 7.25 thinking themselves in good time for the 7.30 start. Their confidence oozed away when the school remained empty and uncharacteristically silent so they headed off to the Waterford, always a good bet for an alternative venue. The hotel failed to match their expectations but at this point they spied Councillor Basil Dunlop's car going through the square. The ubiquitous Basil is always a safe bet for any kind of meeting so they gave chase as far as the YMCA. By the time they breathlessly burst in on the coffee room they were just in time to interrupt the Rev. Morris Smith in the middle of his welcoming prayer. In embarrassed retreat they stumbled out and being now destitute of any better ideas returned to the school where they arrived just in time for the 8 o'clock meeting. We can all sleep easier in our beds in the sure and certain knowledge that we have Grantown's brightest and best looking after our interests.

****

Not that this column is in the market for a car, being happy with the company Porsche, but it recently had to fritter away some time in a motor dealers establishment and idly thumbed through the details of the Renault Spider sports model to discover that advertisers are still capable of mangling the English language in the pursuance of their trade. In describing this exotic sports model it said,
"the vertically opening doors will command additional onlooker admiration."
Make them all sick as pigs is what they mean.

****

HERE COME DE JUDGE. An occasional correspondent with this column is US Judge Bob Armstrong who has an apartment in Aviemore which just goes to prove that even judges can have lapses. He takes us to task because we here on the 10th floor have been ignoring our duties to promote the art of limerick writing.

We used to have regular poetry competitions, if the sort of stuff that fell on our mat could rightly be described as poetry. Bob's distress was such that he neglected to put a stamp on his envelope causing a scurry around the 10th floor's petty cash tin to enable us to prise the letter from our unwilling postie's nerveless fingers. To stir our inert bones he has sent us a short piece of doggerel as follows:

> A limerick is a poem that is funny,
> It helps make a cloudy day sunny,
> But most are risqué
> Which is not always OK,
> But the clean ones are not very funny.

****

Because of his prompting, the entire Foolscap team has decided to have a think-in in my en-suite Jacuzzi to try to come up with a suitably poetic Christmas competition. Using my droit de seigneur, I have elected to sit in the hot tub next to Big Babs. (Why do they call her that?- Ed.) Something awesome should surely come up. Bob has also sent me two jokes which brought a blush to the delicate cheek of our editor. Readers wishing a copy of these jokes should send a stamped addressed envelope to the editor marked "Dirty Jokes" in the top left hand corner. Alternatively we may get round to publishing them in due course.

****

Our angling correspondent Sandy Bennet is perhaps better known as a Traffic Warden or Kingussie's one and only roundabout. Sandy, as our regular readers will immediately realise, is constructed on fairly generous lines. In his official capacity he recently joined a number of local bobbies to take part in the annual Scottish Police Federation Angling Championships at the Lake of Menteith, Scotland's only lake. Older readers will recall that Sandy was the man who booked James Bond for parking a few years ago when Sean Connery was passing through the area. Taking this brave feat and his first class angling knowledge into account the team decided that Sandy was the man for Captain. He delivered the pre match tactical team talk and possibly as a result of this talk to instil a sense of pride, enthusiasm and a lust for prizes, the team failed to catch any fish at all. However Sandy's professional knowledge was put to more practical use when he was given the job of parking the boats. Only one small shadow of doubt clouds the normal probity of this event. Usually each boat has a crew of three and the names for sharing are drawn out of a hat but it is believed that in the interests of safety the draw was nobbled this year to ensure that the two lightest contestant were drawn to share with Sandy.

****

Aviemore's Old Bridge Inn has moved into the new age of technology. The waitresses have all been issued with small paging devices which keep the food moving to the right places at the right time. When a particular order is ready the kitchen staff signal the waitress concerned and the device attached to the girl's belt vibrates. Some particularly coarse customers are claiming that this pub now has the happiest workforce in town. Whatever do they mean?

****

Grantown's perceived problem with its rowdy youth was the subject of a meeting of the Community Council. Provost Charlie Sinclair stood on the stage with black board and chalk and quite reasonably as a starting point, asked the question loudly "Is there a problem?"

As if to prove that indeed there was some sort of a problem the ground immediately opened up old testament style and swallowed the hapless Provost leaving a bewildered group of councillors staring in disbelief. When Charlie dragged himself up through the dusty splintered remains of the stage on which he had so recently stood the well meaning council roared their approval. The meeting failed to find any particular solutions but Charlie has been booked as the star turn for the Christmas Party.

****

Citizens of Aviemore have nothing to fear while the guardians of the law are out and about fighting crime day and night. One of our local heroes has recently been observed sporting a substantial bandage on one wrist. This is the sort of thing that we expect to see from our policeman who are always in the front line at great risk of personal injury but in this case the rozzer concerned has been reticent in explaining how he came by his dreadful wound. His reticence may be the result of quiet professional modesty but on the other hand there may be more to it. This column's investigative crime reporter has discovered the truth. The poor PC got bitten by a fellow policeman's dog whilst patting it on the head. (The dog not, the policeman) Obviously highly trained. (The dog, not the policeman)

****

Down to Kingussie on Sunday 7th to do a little Christmas shopping (two tins of Budweiser and a Spice Girls poster) to discover the main street ablaze with festive cheer, an air of gaiety and what journalists the world over like best, lots of freebies. The town was awash with promenading worthies from up and down the valley. I sampled a cup of Gluhwein at Mostly Pine, or Mostly Wine as it should perhaps be called, while Mrs Foolscap purchased a few interesting items. When I got bored waiting I popped out into the street and was handed a bag of roast chestnuts at Allan's the Chemists where John Allan was roasting his nuts in the open air. A cheery Santa handed out sweeties to the kiddies and as is the habit, it seems, of Santas all over the world, applied himself to some secret elfin brew and got remarkably cheerier as the day wore on.

1998

Rumours of my retirement have been greatly exaggerated. Here I am back again a fact which will cause great disappointment and distress throughout the area. Those of you who count the minutes to each edition of this column will have noticed that our kindly, handsome, witty (That's enough - Ed.) Editor the talented Ken Smith allowed the 10th floor a short leave for the first time in years and needless to say we took it. The Foolscap family also moved house at this unlikely time of year so all in all the time just seemed to slip by. Mrs Foolscap was enjoying the move so much that I hardly liked to interfere and left it all to her. Luckily she didn't notice and as she has the good sense never to read this column, my secret should be safe.

The glad New Year has come around once more with all that it entails. At this time of year the 10th floor traditionally goes in for, what can only be called, excess. Excess in everything that we like and as far as possible avoiding all those things that we don't like. Work for example. Nonetheless, due to some minor virus I was disinclined to allow alcohol to pass my lips although in the best spirit of the traditions which made this country great, I forced itself to have a few. The illness has now passed and I should soon be able to come off solids.

****

That peculiar white stuff which very occasionally falls here and turns this alleged ski resort into complete chaos has struck again. Those caught most completely off guard turned out to be the Chairlift Company whom one might have assumed would be most adept in these conditions. In fairness, however, I suppose since the various staff and management changes they haven't seen much of it. Worse still they managed to strand most of the staff in the process however this column is renowned for its fairness (only on the 10th floor - Ed.) and because every other boot has been put in we will refrain from further comment. But we can occasionally burst into laughter.

Nearby, a hapless visitor to Glenmore Lodge drove up to reception and seeing the car park packed to bursting point enquired where he might deposit his vehicle. He was told that there was extra parking at the rear so he drove round and seeing a nice empty, flat, snow covered area picked his spot and drove in. Unfortunately what he drove into was the canoe practice pond.

The multi million pound electronic signs on the A9 also had a first real trial. Instead of boring us with such witty sayings as "Drive carefully" and "Check your petrol" they had an opportunity to let us know what was happening. As I was driving from Inverness on Tuesday the sign proclaimed "Caution Snow on road at Slochd." When I got to Slochd I discovered that this information was flawed. There was no snow although there was a dead rabbit on the road. I thought of phoning the control desk to inform them that conditions had improved but felt that the notice "Caution dead rabbit on the road at Slochd" lacked some of the dramatic appeal of the original if inaccurate message. The prize for the most useless message was on the sign outside Aviemore. At long last it had its chance to warn us all that the roads were blocked with snow but unfortunately the sign was unreadable . It was completely obliterated by …. er …. SNOW.

****

We here on the 10th floor of Strathie Tower, lounging in luxury around our upmarket suite of offices, often hark back to our youth (What a memory - Ed.) and can still recall those golden summer days when we were boy Scouts and girl Guides. (Were you both?- Ed.) (Yes. But that's another story -Flscp.) Our memories of pleasant if mildly disastrous outings return sharply with stories of such goings on still extant in today's hi-tech efficient world.

The Grantown Guides arranged to visit the Inverness Fire Control Centre last Monday in order to finish off their Fire Safety badges. Parents with cars were pressed into service to provide transport and were each given a map of the route by Guide Leader Yve Mackie who had taken great pains to prepare even going to the extent of using coloured pencils to mark the way for those of the meanest intelligence. This very expression naturally brings us to one of the parents, Grantown worthy, Bill Quirie. Bill was confident that he knew where he was going and eschewed such aids as coloured maps. As a result of his innate sense of direction and confidence in his abilities, Bill got hopelessly lost as did Donna Rennie who had mistakenly put her trust in the car in front. While this pair of motorists toured around Fire establishments in a frantic search for their companions, the others, now happily ensconced in the control room, were observing their erratic progress on the security cameras with great delight and no little amusement. Yve has seldom encountered problems with the girls but is beginning to think that she may have to run some sort of training for the parents to ensure that the Guide company can continue.

****

Dalrachney Lodge Hotel is jumping with sheer delight at being awarded 4 stars by the Scottish Tourist Board. Naturally Helen Swanney and all the staff are delighted at this timely appreciation of their high standards but not everyone is happy. One gloomy face pervades the panelled hallways of this douce establishment. Grant Swanney is not quite as cheery about this development as the others. Grant is renowned for a certain cautiousness in releasing coinage from his grasp and has been heard complaining, "Not another bloody sign to replace." We do feel sorry for poor Grant once again having to spend money especially as he has so recently had to buy himself a new Range Rover.

Judge Bob Armstrong of California and Aviemore has sent in a response to last edition's story which referred to Alan Boxx's mother-in-law in less than flattering terms. Sadly for us the Judge has chosen poetry as his vehicle rivalling only Grantown's Bill Quirie for metre and rhyme.

When I read about mother-in-law jokes
And sinister ideas of some blokes
I was shocked by these stories to the core
With the macabre humour from the 10th floor.

Don't take these thoughts from me too lightly
At this age my pen is not too sprightly
Lines are mostly the same diameter
To scan as iambic pentameter

You should try this for yourself sometime
Keep meter straight and still make it all rhyme
If you're good enough this will be in store
Foolscap will soon be on the eleventh floor.

I should immediately tell Judge Dredd, before our Ken has a seizure, that I have no ambitions to take over the editorial suite upstairs. Au contraire, I prefer my en-suite Jacuzzi to his sauna.

****

My request for ideas for animals which local companies could sponsor for the sake of biodiversity has brought a response from Tom Ramage at the Ossian Hotel in Kincraig. He has sent us the following rather apposite suggestions:

Cairngorm Chairlift Company might more appropriately sponsor the Mayfly (One good day and that's it)

Kingussie Post Office (Prop. Gregor Rimmell) could , of course, sponsor the Grouse.

Speysound Radio might favour the Bat, with that piercing signal which generally goes over our heads. (Probably a reference to Mark & Gareth on Saturday night)

Tom concludes with Clive Freshwater at Loch Insh Boathouse suggesting the Beaver because he is always building one dam thing after another.

****

Driving along the A9 listening to Moray Firth radio I found myself listening to the following advert for the government's New Deal scheme.

"Pauline gave Alan and I a good feeling; so we hired her". Aha! At least now we know what a girl has to do to get a job under New Deal.

****

Harry McKay the well known retired Chairlift Race Manager and renowned fisherman has never fully recovered from the ignominy of allowing his wife Muriel to catch a record breaking salmon on the Spey. Now he has even more from which to recover after he was viewed semi naked on the banks of his favourite river recently.

Luckily for Harry, before calling the police to investigate a flashing incident, our informant saw the rotund piscatorial artist throw himself on the ground kicking his feet in the air. Assuming that Harry was having one of the fits which he usually reserves for the Royal British Legion bar when a certain unnamed team wins, our informant rushed to his aid to find water cascading from his waders. It transpired that the vertically disadvantaged Harry had stepped into the Spey at a point which he thought was 2 feet deep but soon discovered was 5 feet deep.

****

Last week's Strathie had a front page story regarding what the Sunday Post would describe as a 'stushie' over car parking charges in Aviemore. For once I am inclined to agree with Provost Malcolm that it is a bad idea. The argument that it will only displace parking to the free areas - such as the Tesco car park - is a valid one as any regular visitor to Portree can testify since charges were introduced there some months ago. This means that nobody will be able to park near Tesco when they want to shop and that trolleys will have to be pushed across the main road and left in the Council's car park plus all the other problems which one might hope our elected officials were smart enough to anticipate for themselves. Apparently not. The argument that people are used to paying for parking is a valid one and that the charges are not excessive however the displacement theory is a very strong argument against charging. The result will be that the Council car park will become a haven of peace amongst the overcrowded privately owned but

114

free car parks available around Aviemore. Aha, I hear you sigh, but what is the answer to the Highland Council's Car Park Account deficit. First, the figures offered are not too encouraging and I immediately noticed that the costs of policing the parking have not been considered at all. The chances are that, in the long run, it would raise almost no money at all. But never fear. As you might expect from one of the most active brains in the area (Who he? - Ed.) I have been musing on this for some time prior to the stushie. The answer should be obvious to any Council economist of even the meanest intelligence. In Castle Street in Inverness, on a prime development site there is a car park with electric barrier and full time attendant which is reserved for the exclusive use, Monday to Friday, of a select band of Highland Council employees and one must presume is paid for by all we community charge payers. Worse. The man in the cap who operates the barrier is paid by the public to keep the public out and to make sure that only the great and the good pass through to this exclusive city centre parking site which, I may add, is often only half full. Many local people work in Inverness and would be delighted to have such an advantageous parking place for their exclusive use but sadly the good councillors have gradually increased the parking charges and squeezed us further and further out. The answer is simple. This site must be sold forthwith for development and at a stroke it would wipe out the deficit for years to come. Investing the money earned from the sale added to the extra rates that could be charged on the new building would bring in enough to cover such a deficit until the end of time itself or until the first meteor strikes. There should be enough left over to keep a few rural schools open too! And what about the poor Council employees who would have to join us ordinary mortals and drive around Inverness in search of parking places? Oh dear, how sad, never mind.

****

One or two sour faces at the recent opening of Aviemore's recently restored Victorian Railway Station and the start of a new steam service direct from there. Not least were two local ladies who were brusquely refused entry while a substantial group of freeloaders stuffed themselves at our expense. The few local people allowed to attend did so in one official capacity or another. One of these was our undernourished editor Ken Smith. When one of the lucky guests asked why our dogged investigative reporter Linda Jolly was not covering the story, Ken, officiously replied that she was attending the opening of Tor Lodge. Why, the lady enquired, was she covering Tor Lodge while Ken was at the station? "Because there isn't a free lunch at Tor Lodge," came the frank reply.

But our Ken didn't just go for the free lunch. He managed to interview the Steam Railway Company's General Manager, Stephen Wood, between toothsome mouthfuls of sponsored grub. He enquired when the next phase would be opened but at this juncture Stephen's wife Tracy interjected. "From now on everything opens on May the 29th," she said.

"How so?" enquired the editor, careful not to dribble any of his pate de foie gras on the lady's shoes.

116

"Because this is our anniversary and he gets to take me out for a meal at someone else's expense," she replied with a degree of acerbity believed to have been directed at her husband.

****

Maisie Grant of Aviemore made plans to go to the Glasgow Garden Festival this year but, being an avid horticulturist and having attended this floral arrangement in the past, she was worried about the traffic congestion. In previous years the queues of cars attempting to visit the show and the frustration of sitting amongst other motorists in the exhaust filled atmosphere had almost spoiled the occasion for her. This year she had read that Strathclyde police had come up with a new traffic management scheme to help alleviate the distress of the flower folk and was looking forward to a more environmentally friendly visit. As Maisie approached the festival site she was extremely impressed with the speed of traffic and the complete lack of congestion. She was considering writing a flattering letter to the police congratulating them on the success of their operation until she got to Strathclyde Park. That's when she discovered that she had arrived a day early.

****

Hughie Clark, sometime crofter, sometime ski god and occasional bon viveur may have made the fatal mistake of mixing elements from two of the above categories of lifestyle when he was spotted fumbling with his mobile phone in the cab of his tractor.

117

Unfortunately, the mobile accidentally slipped from his grasp, presumably because of a bump in the terrain, and ended up beneath one of the tractor's larger rear wheels where it disappeared without trace. To ensure the accuracy for which this column is justly renowned I have been trying to phone him to verify this story but, somewhat oddly, there has been no reply.

****

The silly season is almost upon us. The time when national newspapers print pointless and foolish stories because the politicians have all gone on holiday. It is a fair indictment on our politicians that, when they are on holiday there is no news. Taking this in conjunction with the old saying "No news is good news," we must come to the inescapable conclusion that our politicians are all bad news to a man. And indeed woman. The point, if there is one, about this long and meaningless preamble is that the Strathie intends to be just as silly as all the other newspapers and it might as well start here. The other reason for a long and meaningless preamble is that it puts up the word count, fills more space and justifies the expense of my new company Porsche.

My Loch Morlich mole has decided that due to some confusion arising out of the moving home of the steam trains the following information should be offered to all visitors.

The steam railway station is now located at the station. The Strathspey railway station is called the Speyside station. The train station is called the Aviemore station. The Aviemore station and the Speyside station are the same place. The new station cannot be called the new station as it is so old that it is a listed building. Access to the station is through the station. Visitors then go over the bridge to the new Speyside station which is old. Don't send visitors through the tunnel as this would take them to the old Speyside station which is closed.

The new station was officially opened last month but since then it has been shut. There has been no new opening at the station but it is now open. It is the old station (not the listed building but the other one) which is now shut.

Don't use the finger signs on the totem poles as they point to the Speyside station (shut) and not the Speyside station (open). The finger signs to the train station are correct so visitors should follow the sign for trains and not the sign for steam trains. The sign outside the station was wrong last week but is right this week.

All trains leave from the station, both steam and diesel except on Saturday when the steam train is a diesel.

OK. Now is everybody clear about that.

****

Those of our readers who managed to drag themselves through the article on his Alaskan fishing trip by our old friend Captain Billy may not have realised that the last paragraph was inadvertently left out. For those who may feel that they did not get the entire benefit of the article I have acquired the missing conclusion which reads as follows:

"If you have to be stuck in the wilderness be stuck with Ted Taylor is what I say.

He could even identify every animal by its faeces, which is just a fancy name for droppings, which in its turn is a euphemism for….

Well you get the idea.

Not a particularly useful skill in Spey Valley you might think. Don't be too sure. I well remember the shock of one morning. As I gazed at the foetid offering, fear brushed my gut and a frisson of terror rippled down my spine. It seemed impossible but almost certainly, within the last few hours, Foolscap had passed this way."

Some nerve. Just as well that it was left out is what I say. Since that article was written, the old sea dog has been back to Alaska for yet another trip and has been up to the 10th floor of Strathie Tower regaling us with tales of his derring-do. Mixing socially with bears as he does in Alaska he reckons that the trip is better for his bowels than a high fibre diet. This time he flew over the Alaskan range to a gold mine in the far north. He stayed in a cabin of the most rustic manufacture which he considers would be lucky to get passed our local building control. The toilet was an outhouse of ridiculously flimsy construction. On the first morning he settled down in the loo with an abridged version of War & Peace when 300 pounds of Black bear padded up with a view to scoffing the household's Labrador pup for its breakfast. The bear returned later and got shot at for his trouble. After that Captain Billy took a .44 revolver with him on all his lavatorial excursions, commenting "He kept me in that dunny for almost half an hour. Now I plan to get my own back."

He also had another type of embarrassing moment when he went to make a purchase and found that his wallet with all his credit cards had completely disappeared. Drinking companions of the wily seafarer will have heard this one before. It seems that his wallet can disappear just as mysteriously every time his round is due.

****

Fans of our ex-photographer Gordon Lennox will be glad to know that he is back in the area snapping away good style although no longer with the Strathie. Gordon recently had a frightening experience every bit as bad as a 300 pound Black Bear. An exotically dressed young lady of extravagant proportions approached him and asked if he would like to photograph her. Gordon showed that willingness for work that is the sign of the dedicated professional. She handed him her business card which suggested all manner of excitements without stating anything too strongly. Everything might have proceeded swimmingly had not the young lady in question announced that she expected our bold lensman to pay her for the privilege of visiting her hotel room and taking a few discreet snaps. Gordon may be a fool but he is not a silly fool. He pointed out that as a professional photographer it was his habit to charge for taking pictures and not pay to take them. The lady was unabashed - probably as a result of many similar disappointments in the past - and merely enquired if he had any friends who might like to take up the offer. Gordon made his excuses and departed quickly but I gather still has her business card if any enthusiasts of photography wish to enquire further.

****

This column - as you would expect - attended the recent beer festival in Aviemore. Having spent the previous weekend in the mud at the Grantown Show, Aviemore's Green seemed altogether grassier although not especially drier. Apparently the event was less than well supported. Part of the trouble may lie in the concept of charging for listening to music in a tent. The flaw in this plan is that the 'sair grippit' can stand outside and listen for free. However there were one or two people who enjoyed themselves enough for all those who missed the occasion. On Saturday night kilted local talent spotter, itinerant musician and false-beard salesman Duncan Stewart lived up to his sobriquet 'Drunken Stupor' and fell off the stage while trying to arrange some sound systems. Almost immediately after this exciting piece of ad lib drama two lads rushed out of the marquee and vomited a considerable quantity of real ale on the lawn. The Sunday was altogether more subdued with a high quality of visitor (i.e. me.) to enjoy the excellent music and the excellenter ale. Naturally thish column sticksh to itsh principlsh and refrainsh from excesh.

Robin Hood may never have existed but the concept of robbing the rich to give to the poor, which is purported to have been his main aim, has always fired our imaginations. The modern day thief has no such scruples or so it would seem. The charity shop in Kingussie had a rather fetching wedding dress on display in the window. There have been no break-ins at the premises, there is always at least one member of staff on duty and the place has no 'back shop' where a staff member could get lost but somehow or other the wedding dress has gone. Disappeared from the window. This may be yet another incidence for Mulder & Scully to investigate. Possibly alien activity is behind the disappearance. Maybe the dress will be returned with only the sketchiest memory of what befell it. However the staff at the charity shop are taking a marginally more pragmatic view. They are watching with interest all the wedding photos in the Strathie in case they recognise their recently purloined stock so our readers are warned. If somebody offers you a wedding dress which fell off the back of a lorry, you are advised to turn it down in case your appearance in the wedding section standing next to your beau is followed by an equally public appearance in front of our young handsome Procurator Fiscal.

****

Grantown's ex bookmeister Bill Quirie has been at it again. Bill is a man with a genius for attracting trouble. For reasons that we cannot, or will not, explain things regularly go wrong for Bill. Because of the nature of this story I fear that readers may jump ahead reaching their own conclusions too early. Sadly, I cannot say that they would be wrong to do so. In spite of that, I tell the story. One day recently Bill was at his housework before departing for work. While he was busy hoovering he noticed that his daughter had neglected to clean out her budgie's cage so bold Bill decided to do over the bottom of the cage with the special budgie cage cleaning attachment which Hoover thoughtfully provide for the animal lovers of this country. Don't get too far ahead now. Bill went to extreme lengths to ensure that the budgie was kept well away from the nozzle throughout the procedure. All would have gone well and according to plan had not a visitor come to the door. In the ensuing confusion surrounding this arrival the Quirie budgie got itself sucked onto to the mouth of the appliance. A horror struck Bill managed to extricate the slightly startled melopsittacus undulatis which according to Bill's own description by now had its wee eyes sticking out like gobstoppers. Readers will be pleased to learn that the budgie is fully recovered and is chirruping away like the very devil. Bill is said to be plying the poor animal with bells, mirrors, ladders and swings in an orgy of repentance.

****

5th November

This is the anniversary of a man whose public spirit knew no bounds. Sadly for us his venture failed and we still have a parliament at Westminster. Even worse, we are going to get one a lot nearer before long. It is worth remembering on this momentous night that the purpose of government is to interfere with and make miserable, the lives of its citizens. So here's to Guy Fawkes who had the right idea but unfortunately lacked the necessary skills.

****

Local star entertainers, The Gilly Brothers, recently returned from their lengthy tour of Denmark (that's three years now and they are still welcomed which says something about Danish musical taste) to promote their latest Album 'Mary's Avenue' a collection mainly written and entirely performed by the musical duo. As part of their wily promotional exercise Fergus persuaded a friend to send several copies of the CD to Radio 2 disc jockey Ken Bruce. The friend being related to the man in question did so having first wrapped the CDs in a copy of The Herald (the other one, not the Strathie) in order to save them arriving decimated into microscopic pieces of plastic. In due course the friend received an email from the renowned music lover and alleged humorous broadcaster which said. "Received your package today. Thoroughly enjoyed its contents. And how thoughtful of you to protect the newspaper with those little boxes."

****

Golf Competition. Why is Carrbridge Golf Club like Maggie Thatcher? Readers are asked for their suggestions and there may be a worthwhile prize for the best suggestions. So far this office has come up with a few of its own. The 10th floor had their own ideas but Ken Smith pre-empted us with his suggestion that they are both tight and very unforgiving. We have another. Our own particular favourite this week is that, like Maggie, the golf club is not for turning. Readers who pass by on their route to Inverness may have observed that a large and unsightly notice has appeared at the entrance saying "NO TURNING." For that reason and no other I drove in for a quick turn round the car park the other day. In the process of doing so I chatted idly with a stander-by who informed me that since the notice had gone up more people than ever had been turning in the car park. Nobody was able to say just why it was felt necessary to erect the notice but all it seems to have done is alert drivers to the possibility that it would be a reasonable place for such a manoeuvre.

As if that wasn't bad enough, golfing adherents of the 10th floor have identified yet another similarity. Both the golf course and Mrs Thatcher have delusions of grandeur. Apart from its pompous plans to turn itself into an 18 hole course this small friendly holiday sporting venue is considering the addition of dozens of new bunkers in order to keep a handful of low handicap players happy. These are the types who find it too easy. As by far the greatest proportion of the 600 membership is made up of hackers perhaps the golfingly disadvantaged should turn up to the AGM en masse and make their feelings known. This column has always wanted a small private golf course of its own and it is only jealous that a few others around here appear to have achieved it.

****

Kingussie is also preparing for the festivities. The merchants of the town are – this week - once again holding their Sunday Open Day to enable the citizenry to catch up on their gift buying and Kingussie shopkeepers to catch up on their overdrafts. Foolscap was amongst those promenading at last year's Open Day and apart from delighting in sampling the free Gluhwein was struck by the cheeriness of their Santa Claus. In fact Santa became so jaunty that he fell over. Normally when shopkeepers advertise for a Santa, one of the main attributes, which they look for, is a bright personality. In a startling departure from the norm and based on the bitter experiences of the past, this year Kingussie traders are looking for a friendly but not terribly cheery Santa. It is in the hope that the day might pass off without incident and the good burghers can maintain their steely grip on reality. Any reader in search of some seasonal excitement should take a trip to Kingussie this Sunday and go Santa spotting. If that doesn't stimulate the passions then surely the sight of John Allan, the chemist, roasting his nuts in the High Street will do the trick.

****

1999

We must have more cheerful news to greet the bright New Year. An anonymous wag has sent a belated entry to the Christmas Poetry Competition unless we have got things wrong and it is an early entry for next year's. He - it does seem to be a he - describes it as "REAL poetry, not those pathetic attempts published on 31st December." "Them's fightin' words mister." I would suggest to our anonymous scribe that he doesn't venture around to Poet's Corner in the Seafield Lodge on a Friday evening and if he does he should not reveal his identity to our two heavyweight entrants who are wont to foregather therein. The word heavyweight here is used in both its literal and metaphoric senses so he should take care. The piece is entitled SKI-FEVER and although he makes no apologies to John Masefield we think perhaps he should.

> I must go down to the Pistes again,
> To those magical runs on my skis,
> And all I ask of McCaskill's jokes,
> Is a day of fine weather please.

I must go up to the hill again,
It's a call I just cannot refuse,
And all I ask is a parking space,
And some method of jumping the queues.

I must go up to the pistes again,
To escape from my dull urban life,
And all I need leave is my answering machine,
And excuses to fob off the wife.

I must go up the A9 again,
To my favourite B & Bs,
And all I demand is an hour in the bath,
And the kitchen to wax my skis.

Poetry is a fine thing, but like rot-gut whisky it should be taken in moderation. Too much can drive a man insane. So it is as a public service that we must sadly draw a veil over the competition and ignore any further offerings of doggerel which may come our way. Unless, of course, anyone feels up to producing something in the style of Burns in time for Rabbie's birthday.

****

Aviemore Photographic's boss, Pavel Satny is renowned for his antipathy towards cars and other mechanical devices. We assume that he does know how to work a camera though. Pavel's interesting parking style is only one of the manifestations of his awkwardness with the motor car. He recently travelled with the family to Inverness to buy a cooker. Before arriving at the electrical superstore of his choice he already had filled the car with a large roll of linoleum. En route the throttle had been sticking and so arriving in the store car park Pavel, with all the family and the linoleum squashed in the car, wanted to find what was causing the problem. He opened his door and leaned out to look underneath blipping the throttle as he did so. Sadly at this point he fell out and the car ran over him. With the car now heading for a brick wall, the family desperately tried to reach around the linoleum to get at the handbrake. Later, looking a bit like a red haired Worzel Gummidge, Pavel in torn sweater, limping and a trifle scuffed insisted on proceeding to the shop. His wife Monica felt obliged to explain to the puzzled assistants, "you'll have to excuse him he's just been run over by a car." Luckily she left out the bit about him also being the driver.

****

Our old friend and Grantown's depute poet laureate Captain Billy has been travelling yet again. (What do retired sea captains do to pass the time after a lifetime of roaming the world? Answer. They roam the world.) Recently he has been to the Azores and has returned with the instructions from the back of his hotel room door. Well I suppose it's better than pinching the towels. One thing we all love is to laugh at foreigners struggling with our language and so we reprint the sheet for you below absolutely verbatim spelling mistakes and all.. The old sea dog who has learned over a lifetime of entering foreign ports that cautious diplomacy pays off wants it to be known that although he found the following amusing he does not intend to mock. After all their English is a better than his Portuguese.

IN CASE OF FIRE FOLLOW THE INSTRUCTIONS
- React without panic in a calm and determined way.
- Don't waste time taking value.
- Look for a free danger position and inform immediately the reception.
- Undress yourself immediately out of the building. (Gerard Hoffnung's French widow in every bedroom could liven things up here.)
- On leaving each room always close the doors
- Don't intervene in the evacuation action or against the fire without being qualified.
- On reaching the outside of the building you should not come back into it.

MEASURES FOR THE PREVENTION OF FIRE
- When you watch some irregularity many set or different equipment to the guests using inform immediately the reception.
- Don't smoke in the bed or even a sofa if you feel sleepy.
- Don't put into the garbage the fag-end just fineshed smoking.
- Don't carry into rooms inflammable products or tools capable to cause fire.

- If there was difficulty to contact the reception dial directly to the firemen by the phone 22333.

****

The Aviemore lager louts are up to their old tricks again. The usual suspects were involved in a trip to watch Saint Johnstone play Dundee United and decided to travel by train. It would be unkind to name names but let us just say that it involved an hotelier, a consultant, a plumber and a Provost. It was less loutish - or for that matter lagerish - than usual as those involved had invited along their wives and sweethearts (two each? - Ed.). Scotrail had very sensibly taken the precaution of removing the bar from the train and although our friends are not so foolish as to travel without some essential supplies, they had been relying on the Scotrail bar as backup. It resulted in the discovery of a use for mobile phones other than the irritation of one's fellow passengers. On discovering Scotrail's omission the hotelier concerned panicked, grabbed his mobile and phoned his friend Don Lawson of Johnny Foxes. Don also has an hotel in Pitlochry and was able to order essential rations to be delivered to the station platform in Pitlochry to await the arrival of our parched and delirious friends. Luckily due to this speedy intervention none of the party died of thirst on the long and gruelling journey to Perth.

****

Here on the 10th floor we are always hanging out other people's dirty washing (well, amusing washing) for all the world (or at least that portion of it that reads the Strathie) to see. Never let it be said that we hide our own silly light behind a bushel. At a recent evening in Grantown, Foolscap was invited to address a group of people but neglected the simple precaution of observing rule one when in front of a multitude. Thus it was that I stood up, moved into the spotlight to start talking and at this point, several moments too late, I checked my zip and sadly found it gaping open. Luckily the sight caused no excitement among those present - as indeed it never has done - and was smartly adjusted without too much fuss. It seems that I may be heading down the erratic path recently followed by our confused editor as, a few days later, I drove casually through a red traffic light in Inverness. Luckily no one in authority was watching. In my defence I had just returned from a few days in Orkney where the concept of a traffic light, or indeed traffic, has yet to be accepted; so possibly I am not losing that essential stranglehold on reality so necessary for a columnist of international standing.

****

Technological advancement has also brought some email to us on the subject of the Millennium Bug or Y2k compliance as we technophiles call it. Our informants tell us that due to Year 2000 compliance problems the new Microsoft operating system, Windows 2000, will not now be available until February 1901.

Another item came in from distant Nairn. From it we learn that the following scroll, dated 1 BC, was recently discovered and translated:

Dear Cassius,

Are you still working on the Y-Zero-K problem. This change from BC to AD is giving us a lot of headaches and we haven't got much time left. I don't know how many people will cope with working the wrong way round. Having been working happily downwards for ever, now we have to start thinking upwards. You would think that someone would have thought of it earlier and not left it to us to sort out at the last minute. I spoke to Caesar the other evening. He was livid that Julius hadn't done anything about it when he was sorting out the calendar. He said he could understand why Brutus turned nasty. We called in Consultus, but he simply said that continuing downwards using minus BC won't work and, as usual, charged us a fortune for doing nothing useful. Surely we will not have to throw out all the tablets and start again? Macrohard will make yet another fortune selling new clay tablets out of this I suppose. And we only installed Tablet II a year ago. Imperial Business Mechanisms are insisting that unless all the abacuses have new beads, they won't support them next year. The moneylenders are paranoid of course! They have been told that all the usury rates will invert and that they will have to pay their clients to take out loans. It's an ill wind... As for myself, I just can't see the sand in the hourglass flowing upwards. We have been told of three wise men in the East who have been working on the problem but unfortunately they won't arrive until it's all over. I have heard rumours that there are plans to stable all the horses at midnight at the turn of the year as there are fears that they will all stop and try to run backwards, causing immense damage to chariots and possibly some loss of life. Some say the world will cease to exist at the moment of transition. Anyway, we are still working on this blasted Y-Zero-K problem. I will send an e-scroll to you if anything further develops. If you have any ideas please let me know.

Plutonius

****

Isn't technology wonderful?   Now that we have the Strathie regularly in colour where will it all end?   I am already posing in my en-suite Jacuzzi here on the 10th floor of Strathie Tower while ace photographer Gordon Lennox tries to get a modest shot of my attributes (or should that be 'a shot of my modest attributes'). I am hoping this will be my breakthrough into our new page three photos of glamour persons.   Something for everyone to look forward to.

****

The continuing saga of the Aviemore Centre wallows on its way to oblivion. Observers may be forgiven for a touch of cynicism on reading last week's front-page story regarding the "Developers race to secure funds." Watch those developers go like the highly trained tortoises that they are. So far the race has taken a little over 4 years altogether although depending where you want to start it can go back as far as 1982. The stop press on this story is that part of the application has already been withdrawn but I don't expect that will come as much of a surprise to even our most gullible readers. Various interesting aspects of the current application are of concern including the simple but inescapable fact that the Aviemore Plan – a model of which still sits out in front of the Partnership offices - is now no more than a fiction in spite of the fact that it cost hundreds of thousands of pounds in fees and time spent on consulting throughout the valley. Another more entertaining point is that for many years the Four Seasons Hotel has borne the brunt of aesthetic criticism as being like a sore thumb sticking up out of a Highland scene. Personally I always think it is good to be able to see exactly where Aviemore is from any point of the district but it does tend to meet with considerable public opprobrium. If we are to believe the reports, some intellectually challenged planner has decided that to foil this criticism, the answer is to insist on another tall building (six storeys) with the purpose of, and here I must quote, "forming a node to match the Four Seasons Hotel". So it's official now. Two wrongs DO make a right.

EDUCATIONAL NOTE: **Node,** *n. a knot: a knob or lump: a point of intersection of two great circles of the celestial sphere: a*

meeting place of lines: a complication in a story.
I think I'll go for the complication in a story. It sounds the most likely.

****

This is a momentous week in the fortunes of the Strathie. Readers have marvelled for years at the palatial surroundings in which we have toiled. As if the excesses of our present lifestyle – en-suite spa bath, steam room, marble lined halls and gold fittings throughout – were not enough, we are to move to even more sumptuous accommodation at long last. Strathie Tower's eleven floors are being taken over by the Tourist Office and the building may be renamed. We are moving to the all-new Strathie Tower which is 12 storeys high and has a much larger footprint. (technical term meaning that it takes up more space on the ground)
Naturally we journalists have demanded the very minimum of acceptable office standards such as plunge pools, personal gymnasia, and much, much more. The new and considerably enlarged editorial suite will be on the top floor and our gorgeous, pouting editor, Ken Smith will have access to his own personal roof garden with built in driving range. Sadly this may result in some discomfort for Grantown residents as they go about their domestic concerns in the High Street. When Ken is deep in thought planning the layout of the front page, a steady rain of cheap golf balls will hail down on the passing parade possibly causing some injury. Having watched him play and assuming that he will be aiming for the Square, it seems likely that the square will be the safest place to sit and contemplate the world while Ken's erratic

balls drop all over other parts of town. This is especially piquant as the company whose site we have taken over is the Moray Glass Company. If they had Ken golfing from the roof garden earlier they may have found it worth staying in Grantown.

The Foolscap team have decided to remain on the 10th floor in order to avoid confusion and also to get away from the steady irritating thump as Ken takes divots out of the roof. Now that he will be on the 12th floor of the new building we have gained an extra floor of insulation between us. The new building is only a few yards up the high street and we assume that the 12 storeys will merely act as a node to the existing Strathie Tower and keep the planners happy.

****

Regular readers may recall the tale of the 'Mince King of Kinchurdy Road'. The title fell to Ian Strain, whose small hotel Glenavon is justly renowned for its cuisine. It was given to him on a recent occasion when he made a substantial purchase of mince at throwaway prices in the Aviemore Tesco store. The title is gone. Not to another but it has been superseded by a title based on even greater commercial acumen and tales of cunning, derring-do and negotiation in the exciting world that is food provision today. The good Colonel will henceforth be known as the Asparagus King of Kinchurdy Road because of the following story. He was shopping in a supermarket in Inverness looking for some exotic vegetable to enhance a particular piece of his culinary skill for a group of discerning diners when he noticed that the store was offering asparagus tips at £1.99, Special Offer - 2 for the price of 1. Ian was mulling over the possibilities that this might open up when an operative came along and repriced them at all at 79 pence. Ian Strain is not rash when matters financial are concerned so he added a cautious 2 packs to his trolley just to find out if the offer still operated. For those who do not understand the vagaries of supermarket administration let us digress for a moment. In the case of special offers and for stocktaking purposes, it is the convention to charge both items out and then refund one at the end and this is what happened to Ian. Two were charged out at 79 pence and one was refunded at £1.99 – giving a net profit of 41 pence to the already substantial Strain coffers. Like a well oiled military operation, Ian packed the stuff in his car and then, naturally, went back to clean out their entire stocks of Asparagus. The net result was that on his second visit to the checkout he had 25 packs of Asparagus and the checkout girl had to give him a fiver to take them away.

****

This column attracts a wide-ranging and intellectual readership and as a result the Strathie is a greatly sought after blatt. Recently a lady entered our palatial new offices anxious to acquire a newspaper. Shona Donald, whose 'Auntie Wainright' sales techniques are justly renowned in Grantown and beyond informed her that she should hand over 36 pence and take one. The woman hesitated, eyeing the Foolscap logo, then said "All I really wanted was a paper to wrap my fish in to take it home."

Things are slack up here on the 10th floor. With Editor Ken Smith out of the office for a few minutes I pop up to his roof garden on the 12th floor to practise my golf swing but unfortunately put the first ball through Mortimer's front doorway and the second bounces past the Co-op into oblivion. I turn my mind to a recent press release which announces – and not before time in my opinion – that red meat is, once again, good for us. The next shock. Friday's newspapers were full of the findings of one group that sunshine – which used to be good for us and then became very bad for us – has returned to being beneficial again. However, scan the piece as I might I can find no reference to beer and loose women coming off the danger list as yet so to enhance my healthy hedonistic lifestyle I'll just have to soldier on with a plate of mince and tatties out in the garden.

One Tuesday morning recently, before 9am, our Editor's wife was outside her home speaking to another young woman of a certain age when a mini-bus arrived and young athletic chap hopped out and proceeded to strip off his clothes stopping only when he reached his briefs. Never having seen anything remotely like it before both watched for a moment or two then hurried on their way in pensive mode. Later, still thoughtful, the two ladies conversed and wondered whether they ought to inform Grantown's finest. Later that morning the police duly appeared and having rounded up the lone suspect encouraged him to help with their enquiries. The suspected sex offender turned out to be the Norwegian manager of a Spanish Orienteering team (don't ask) innocently getting on the right clothing to go into the woods and put up signs for an event. Being Norwegian he had no notion that Grantonians take a dim view of people who strip off in public. The citizens of Grantown only getting down to their underwear in private and then only on special occasions such as the Queen's Birthday and Christmas. This column was instantly on the scene near the woods but it seems that the liberal male Norwegian views, sadly, did not spread to the Spanish female orienteers.

****

Paul Lawrie's win at the Open Championship will stir the hearts of Scotsmen in this the year of the first Scottish Parliament for 300 years and take us closer to living the famous line "to be a nation again". Bravehearts to a man, or indeed, woman. But putting all that sentimental, jingoistic claptrap aside for a moment we have momentous news for golfing readers of the Strathie. We have in our midst a sort of Golf Champion. Our very own sylph-like editor, Ken Smith, announced publicly that he had once played golf with the very same Open Champion, Paul Lawrie, and more to the point beat him soundly. In fairness to Paul, further

141

questioning elicited the fact that this happened some considerable time ago when the lad was only 16 years old. Nonetheless, hackers must take their plaudits when they can so Ken is naturally making much of this minor win. The news excited great comment around the editorial suite on the 12th floor of The Herald Building and fans of our robust editor swarmed around him to be regaled with fanciful stories illustrating his feats of prowess on the links. A Foolscap mole asked tentatively, "Have you ever played golf with Paul since that day?" Our editor rounded on the poor mole and vigorously assailed him with the following justification, " Would you play golf with someone who swears and curses at every hole, who drinks copiously and cheats at every opportunity?" "No, of course not," squeaked our terrified mole. Whereupon a voice from the throng said, "Neither would Paul Lawrie."

****

Like current television programme schedulers this column seems to have been reduced to navel gazing. Instead of looking outside for stories we content ourselves with sitting in luxury on the 10th floor reporting on our colleagues. Sadly for us all here and a selection of young nubile ladies in the Kingussie area, our man in the soft hat with the press card, Gavin Musgrove is soon to leave us to advance his career and move on to an even larger circulation organ. He is going to work in the Inverness office of the Press & Journal but will maintain his love-nest in Aviemore for the time being. Gavin is amongst that happy band of local inhabitants who have landed parts in the TV series "Monarch of the Glen" currently being filmed near Loch Laggan. To complete his transformation and to allow him to 'really get into the role' Gavin was obliged to put on Highland Dress. As a 'Geordie' his knowledge of, and experience with, kilts is well below the plimsoll line so the wardrobe people installed him in the garment and left him to ponder. After a while Gavin felt the need to visit the Gentlemen's location Portaloo. Only inside did his unfamiliarity with the wrappings around his nether regions begin to fray the edges of his confidence. As he didn't know quite how to work the contraption, he decided to take it off altogether. Very sensible in the short term but after he had concluded his affairs he discovered that he had no idea how to re-assemble his costume. At this point in the story he was loudly paged for his scene and had to shout for help. At present we have heard nothing of how the matter was resolved but mental pictures of Gavin appearing wearing only a sporran have put several staff members off their afternoon tea already.

****

Willie Stewart is one of Aviemore's favourite ex-policemen. However his penchant for schadenfreude has occasionally coloured some people's view of this honest copper. (Educational Note: Schadenfreude is a German word meaning 'to take pleasure in the misfortunes of others.' Curiously no other nation has felt it necessary to coin a word for this particular emotion.) Willie, or Dubbie as he has been affectionately known since his childhood in Boat of Garten, may have inadvertently offered his many friends a little chance of enjoying retribution. Recently Dubbie took the opportunity to trim a few of his garden trees and scaled the dizzy heights to perform a little arboreal topiary. Unfortunately for him his ladder became unstable and Dubbie was precipitated into his ornamental fishpond causing a waterspout that was clearly seen as far away as the Alt na Craig. When he surfaced cut, bruised and spitting exotic species of fish, he was further dismayed to discover that his wife Ann, far from rushing to comfort him in his hour of need, was doubled up convulsed with laughter. Curiously for one who has taken such pleasure from the misfortunes of others, Dubbie entirely failed to see the funny side of this experience.

****

Those of our readers who wish to enrol the support of their local councillor may think twice if that councillor happens to be Angus Gordon and the matter needing support requires keen perception. Councillor Gordon's powers of observation were put to the test recently and found wanting. Last week the Rotary Club ran an Antiques Roadshow when one and all were invited along to bring their prize collections and have them valued by local experts. The great and the good arrived laden with their treasures and bric-a-brac. Angus's wife brought along a painting to get the expert once-over but when the good councillor saw this work of art he exclaimed.

"Here, that's a nice painting. Where did you find that?" To this apparently reasonable question Mrs Gordon gave her husband a withering look before replying,

"It's been hanging above the fireplace for the last twenty years".

144

****

RSPB wardens have been taking down deer fences around the Abernethy forest in order to return the habitat to Mother Nature's care and very laudable the exercise is too. Their fondness for natural habitat however does not seem to extend to their own gardens where my Nethy moles have spotted a curious tendency. Fences around the gardens of many local RSPB staff have… Yes, you've guessed. Deer proof fences.

Author's Note

The works of Foolscap are wondrous to behold but couldn't be accomplished without the help of my many moles. These tireless creatures work away quietly digging the dirt on the great and the good of Badenoch, and for that matter, Strathspey. In short, the area covered by our favourite blatt, The Strathie, or to give it it's Sunday name, The Strathspey and Badenoch Herald, the very newspaper in which all these pieces first appeared.

I had intended to thank all those who have given me information over the years but was struck by two particular thoughts that paused me in my manly stride. First, I couldn't remember all their names and cannot therefore put in those that I remember for fear of offending those I have forgotten. Second, it may be that many of my moles are less than anxious to be fingered, as informants, in quite such a public fashion. It is just possible that old wounds have yet to heal and that my less genteel readers may feel that a taste of retribution is what these people need.

With this particular threat in the forefront of my mind and in spite of a great desire to swank about pretending to be a great author, I have decided that I must also remain anonymous. Some of the victims of my pen may be out there in the shadows just waiting their chance to strike and so the world's greatest columnist must stay safe and hidden, ever vigilant against the oppression of our political masters. (Is this good stuff or what?) (What? – Ed)

Which reminds me. Thanks, Ed. We both know that the column would never have achieved such global appeal without your learned interjections.

Foolscap

October 1999

10th Floor
Strathie Tower
High Street
Grantown-on-Spey

146